GRACEDBYGRIT

THE ENTREPRENEURIAL WOMAN'S GUIDE TO STARTING A BUSINESS WITH POWER, PASSION & PURPOSE

Kimberly Caccavo and Kate Nowlan

Published by Best Seller Publishing®, Pasadena, CA
Best Seller Publishing® is a registered trademark
Printed in the United States of America.

Most Best Seller Publishing® titles are available at special quantity discounts for bulk purchases for sales promotions, premiums, fundraising, and educational use. Special versions or book excerpts can also be created to fit specific needs.

For more information, please write:
Best Seller Publishing®
1346 Walnut Street, #205
Pasadena, CA 91106
or call 1(626) 765 9750
Toll Free: 1(844) 850 3500
Visit us online at: www.BestSellerPublishing.org

Dedication

To Jim, whose generous spirit, kind intelligence and business guidance helped us turn our dream into a reality.

To each of our kids: Maggi, Christopher, Gwen and Grace. Thank you for sharing your moms and helping us by modeling, selling and photographing our clothes. We are grateful and recognize the sacrifices you endured so we could follow our passion and purpose.

To our parents. We are each lucky to have strong inspirational parents that gave us the confidence to embrace our grit and realize the grace within.

Contents

Preface

Are you thinking of starting a business or a nonprofit? Do you have a project or dream that is itching to take form? Are you afraid to try? Afraid your idea isn't good enough? Afraid that you'll fail? If your answer is "yes" to any of these questions, you've picked up the right book.

We are the founders of **GRACEDBYGRIT** and, fortunately for you, we've already dragged ourselves through the venture jungle and the haze of the startup battlefield and we're here to give you the final push you need to create something that allows you to live your life with passion and purpose. We believe that you can start and grow a business by developing your grit, recognizing your grace, and harnessing the power of giving.

Throughout our journey, we (Kimberly Caccavo and Kate Nowlan, pleased to meet you!) have been privileged to meet every day with gritty, graceful women from all walks of life. We are all pursuing our dreams, and, for many of us, the hurdles are great. Each time another woman is gracious enough to share her story we are inspired and amazed. Each day is a chance to remember that women are strong, women are powerful, and women can not only overcome, we can trailblaze!

We are going to share the stories of some of these remarkable women. Whatever the hurdles, these women have shown they can make things happen. All you need is a road map and grit; did we mention grit? We want to instill in you, our readers, the recognition that, "If she can do it, I can too"! We will provide you with the tools you'll need as you pursue that dream, whether it be a single fundraising event, a nonprofit organization or a new business. Whatever your passion, we know it's born of a deeply personal experience and, in many cases, a clear call to action from within your soul. We know you won't rest until you've turned your idea into action. We understand: we're moms and entrepreneurs; it feels as if we haven't rested for years!

Our Story

We have worked together since 2010, when our relationship was as athletic trainer and trainee. Kimberly told Kate, "If my butt looked like yours, I would run every day also. What I need is a legging with LOTS of compression and a GREAT design." This was the beginning of a conversation that, at the time, we had no idea would lead to a business partnership. As Kate pushed Kimberly harder than seemed possible, the conversation continued. "There must be a better way to carry your phone while you run," Kate said as she punished Kimberly up four flights of stairs. We talked about what we would do if we could create the perfect running and athletic apparel. We decided including a whistle would be good so that you could scare off a would-be attacker and call for help. Sun protection was also a must. But, it was just talk—a way to get through the training session. We had lots of ideas about what we would like in our own athletic apparel.

One day, at the end of a run, one of us joked, "We should start our own company and make athletic clothes that make women look and feel great; they'll perform better." It was an off-handed comment that wouldn't leave us alone for the next few years.

Starting a business together didn't seem possible. Kate was a single mother in her thirties with two girls in elementary school. Kimberly was a working mom in her fifties who also had two children in school.

How could two busy moms start a business? It seemed like just a pipe dream.

It wasn't until 2013, two and a half years later, that we sat down at a computer, wrote the business plan and together we incorporated our business.

We were good at listening to each other, and we wanted to build a company for women, by women. We surveyed hundreds of women about their interest in athletic apparel brands and what features they looked for in workout clothing. What did actual women want in terms of colors, fit, safety features, and durability? This might seem like an obvious step, but there is a stunning gap between what *you* think your customers want, and what they actually want. This process revealed that athletic apparel companies were overlooking a feature that women wanted and needed. Overwhelmingly, we heard that women wanted fitness wear built for performance *and* safety. Safety? That was not an obvious feature of any apparel company we had seen before. Women wanted fabric that gave them high ultraviolet protection, and was quick-dry, soft, and luxurious. It needed to wash well, and it needed to come in classic colors that could supersede trends. Plus, women wanted a pocket that held their phone. A clear picture of our customer was painted: she was timeless, elegant, worked hard, and needed clothes that could keep up with her.

Next came the fun stuff, the culture of the business. Our vision wasn't just about apparel. So many women we know turned to sport, exercise, and world travel to overcome trauma or life obstacles, with the understanding that developing their capacity for physical endurance would also build their mental and emotional strength. We wanted to inspire women (and girls) to arrive at a fuller realization of their power and purpose through fitness, as we and other women we'd met had done. We wanted to create an engaged community of women who supported one another and provided an infrastructure where they could turn in times of need.

Next, we looked at the athletic apparel market. Was there room for a new brand? We discovered that no one was focused exclusively on women in this sector. How would we differentiate ourselves? What would we call ourselves? That was one of the hardest decisions.

Here is where it got personal.

We had each experienced a major life event that forced us to learn what we were truly made of. We were sure we weren't alone in this. Every woman has a gritty moment that could make or break her, and how we make it through those moments define us. Grit is often what gives us grace. It seemed so obvious: **GRACEDBYGRIT**.

We loved the name because grace and grit seemed to be words from opposite ends of the spectrum. Yet, they are complementary.

Grace is a beautiful word. It conjures an image of physical, elegant beauty. We are all beautiful in body by virtue of the miracle of life. But more importantly, it's a word that speaks to an inner spiritual beauty.

Grace is rising above.
Grace is humility.
Grace is serenity.
Grace is peace.
Grace is acceptance.
Grace is kindness to others and yourself.

Grit seems diametrically opposed to grace. It brings to mind hard-bitten pioneers, hardscrabble livelihoods, and hard-knock life experiences, but it is a quality we all have at different times, whoever and wherever we are.

Grit is strength.
Grit is discipline.
Grit is honor.
Grit is trustworthiness.
Grit is doing the right thing in the face of wrong.

In writing this book, we set out to make these wonderful words the context for an exploration of grit. We aim to show how—as strong, independent women—we can all cultivate grit to find our grace, and we have filled these pages with inspirational stories of real women who have done just that.

We hope that we can reach women who have perhaps been considering making a meaningful change in their lives but felt something holding them back. Even if we encourage only one of you to stand up, shake down, and chase your dream over fields, mountains, or oceans, then our book will have served its purpose.

Yours in grit,

Kimberly and Kate

Part I:

GRACE

CHAPTER 1

Guts

Starting a business or project that honors what you are passionate about is hard. Really hard. We know this from past and current experience. The mortality rate of startup businesses is alarmingly high and, according to the US Bureau of Labor Statistics, only 50 percent survive five years[1]. We haven't seen any statistics for female-founded startups, but we are willing to bet that the rate might be higher— not because women are less capable but because they face greater challenges (more on that later!).

A number of these startup fatalities can be attributed to poor entrepreneurial skills, but not all of them. The reality is that the marketplace is a fickle master who is benevolent one moment and heartless the next. Competition is fierce, economic confidence is low, and consumers are more powerful than ever. It's a tough, tough world out there right now for the entrepreneurial dreamer. We knew that when we started, and we are even more sure of it now. That knowledge, however, is not a deterrent for us: it's more like a red rag to a bull.

Like most entrepreneurs, the day we started our business, we were excited and nervous. We knew that our product and story were great, the market was huge, and we could make our dreams come true. (Kate had the *Laverne and Shirley* theme song playing in the background.) What wasn't to like? Our vision was clear, and our business plan was solid. We had a strong brand and a way to produce the goods. We were

---

[1]   https://www.fool.com/careers/2017/05/03/what-percentage-of-businesses-fail-in-their-first.aspx

ready to hit the ground running—we were warmed up, pumped up and standing on the starting line. We thought we could easily get funding.

Wow. Were we wrong! It was NOT easy at all.

First, we went to a local group of "angel investors." Angels are aptly named; they are people who like to get in on the ground floor of any business opportunity and give you help when you are too small to get traditional investors. As first on board, their risk is higher, but their potential reward is greater. This particular group consisted of about thirty men and one woman, who all sat in a large conference room. Perhaps alarm bells should've been ringing at this point, but we were buoyant and excited to share our vision with them. We were ready to pass a metaphorical hat around for those who couldn't wait to throw their money at us right then and there.

In our pitch, we told them the name of our business, **GRACED**BY**GRIT,** and why we chose that name. We told them how every woman has a gritty moment and how she gets through it becomes her grace. We told them that all women have been graced by grit and a lot of us use sports and athletics to get through difficult times in our lives. We then delivered our business plan in their required format, passed around our clothing samples, and concluded our presentation. Job done. Pitch perfect.

Silence.

Were they simply rendered speechless by our brilliance? Finally, someone spoke up. Phew! At last! Maybe they just needed someone to uncork the bottle…

"Is there room for another athletic apparel company?"

We quickly shared what we knew about the large size of the market.

"Is the market big enough?"

We showed that there was indeed room in the market for our brand.

"Do you really think women will buy another pair of leggings?"

*"Women won't relate to '**GRACED**BY**GRIT**.' You need to change the name."*

And then the final feedback directed toward Kate:

"You have really nice legs. My suggestion would be that you stand in front of the podium and not behind it when presenting in the future."

We probably blinked in unison, momentarily stunned.

A few questions later, another man added (perhaps because he didn't want Kimberly to feel inadequate about the shapeliness of her legs):

"And you have a great smile, Kimberly. Maybe you should smile more when you give your presentation."

More blinking from us as we thought, *If you smile when you're delivering hard business figures, wouldn't it seem somewhat disingenuous?!*

They passed on the opportunity, of course.

One of the leaders met us in the hallway. He told us how he had started a successful women's athletic apparel company twenty years prior. He liked the idea, but he was investing in a competing women's triathlon brand.

As we remember that experience, it is easy to believe the hard data on the imbalance between the amounts invested in male enterprise versus female enterprise. Research from PitchBook shows that in 2017, only 2.2% of venture capital investment went to women-led businesses. That's $1.9 billion for women compared to $85 billion for men.[2]

We left that meeting and reviewed our business plan, looked at the clothing, created another survey (using SurveyMonkey, a very useful tool) and made sure that our product and name was something we really believed in. We were on the right path, and that gang of hell's angels made us realize that we needed to prove them wrong, so we started setting goals, undaunted by the negativity.

It paid off. Two years later, when we opened our first store, the fellow who led that investors' group, a long-time veteran of the sports apparel industry, invited us for coffee. We met him, and he opened with, "I just want to tell you I'm sorry. I was wrong, and you guys really did it. I'm so amazed that you stuck to it and you made your dream a reality." He added, "Actually, women love your name. It resonates with my wife. She really identifies with it." He was very apologetic and recognized the mistake that the men in that room had made. He acknowledged that we were hard workers, had identified a market niche and had made a business by building a strong group of engaged women. Vindication! What he was saying was "you've got guts, girls." It felt good.

So, what does it mean to have "guts"?

We believe that "guts" refers to a characteristic that can be described as:

- ☐ Acting on instinct
- ☐ Persevering to a plan
- ☐ Confronting fears
- ☐ Making things happen

---

[2] https://pitchbook.com/news/articles/do-female-founders-get-better-results-heres-what-happened-when-i-tried-to-find-out (Accessed May 2018)

☐ Working hard

☐ Doing the hard work regardless

☐ Remaining undaunted by criticism (seems to be the moral of the story you tell here)

Sticking It Out

Your dream is a block of marble. You need the tenacity to chip away at it every single day to turn it into a beautiful monument to your soul. Having guts is about accepting failure, learning from it and continuing to try. Sometimes being gutsy is about fighting against yourself or naysayers to achieve what you know in your heart to be right (something we'll return to in the "Reason" chapter).

For an enterprise of any kind to survive beyond those critical first three years, it's essential to have perseverance. Of course, you need to have all your business ducks in a row, but regardless of how prepared you are to launch your idea in a practical sense, you will likely fail without the guts to power through the inevitable humps. We both believe that success is not a straight line. Sometimes you hit a bump in the road; you fall, you head in the wrong direction... but you stop, analyze, and pivot so that you can keep moving towards your goal. *If at first you don't succeed, try, try again.*

Think about those early pioneers who headed west, those men and women who took the long, perilous journey that led to their American Dream. They all made a plan and loaded their wagons with supplies for every eventuality they could think of. Nevertheless, their success was down to two things that couldn't be packed into a trunk: luck and guts. If they were lucky, the conditions were right for their journey and their supplies lasted. But if they were unfortunate, they would need to draw upon pure will and ingenuity to succeed. Today, thankfully, you'll never need the kind of guts (literal and figurative) of the infamous Donner Party who had to resort to cannibalism to survive, but that level of determination is exactly what we're talking about: doing whatever it takes to make your dream a reality. The sacrifice is real and different for everyone.

However, nobody set out to cross the wilderness in a wagon without a plan. It's not necessarily gutsy to simply jump into something; it's foolish! On the other hand, it's not gutsy to stick stubbornly to your guns. Even though your vision remains fixed, you'll need some practical flexibility built into your plan if you're going to weather any storm that hits you. Do you need an MBA to come up with a business plan? Kimberly has one—it didn't hurt! But there are many resources available on the internet, including business plan templates, that are super useful.

You will probably need an expert or two to review your plan at some stage, but whatever your business background, you can start creating an initial proposal that lays out your core idea, your mission, and how you're going to bring the idea to fruition (even if that's just a list of people you need to find to plug your knowledge gaps). This applies to any enterprise—a new nonprofit, an organization or even a one-off event. You can do the first part of the planning yourself, which is the research. Go out and talk to people about your idea, but don't be protective of it for fear that someone might steal it. They won't, because they won't have the passion for it that you do. Create a survey; send it to ALL your friends and their friends. Talk, talk, talk. Ask, ask, ask. People want to help. Everyone has ideas, many of which are good. Then get a great business planning template [3] [4] and some good friends with whom to discuss the idea.

---

[3]   We used https://www.liveplan.com/. BusinessPlan Pro. It was expensive.

[4]   https://www.sba.gov/ These guys were the first. It is sometimes unwieldy to use their site, but the resources are free.

Primal Instinct

Appropriately, having guts is about trusting *your* gut. Don't let your idea get stuck at the gate because you got hung up on the market research and let your findings discourage you. Sometimes, there is no data to support what you want to do, so you just have to do it.

Some of the greatest business ideas were born from a gut feeling—an instinct that something needs fixing. That's exactly what we felt when we came up with **GRACEDBYGRIT**, and it's the essence of "disruption," which has become a ubiquitous business term in recent years. The high-profile disruptors are in Silicon Valley, but we consider ourselves disruptors too, because we went against the grain and did something in a unique way. Just as there were cars called taxis offering rides before there was Uber or Lyft, there were plenty of apparel companies before we came along. The difference was that none of our forebears wanted to serve women in the way we wanted to. Some of our biggest mistakes during the course of our business happened when we ignored our guts, but some of our biggest successes have come when we've listened to them.

We believe you'll get gutsier the more you deliberately put yourself out there and face your deepest fears, rather than hide from them. This is one facet of courage, which we will return to in more detail in a later chapter.

The more you confront your insecurities and fears, the more practice you will gain in overcoming them—and you will almost always overcome them because things are rarely as terrifying or impossible as they may appear. By knowing that you have the ability to overcome something, your confidence grows. You can take bigger risks and say, "How bad could it actually be?" The sooner you have that perspective, the more able you are to face other challenges in your life head on and to know that you can push through them or that you can pivot.

If you combine guts with a strong plan, you can get to the next step faster. Use your guts to say, "I WILL do it." Develop a plan so that each task seems more achievable. It's all about trusting yourself, being strong and moving forward.

Each of our respective children have played soccer, and one thing we've learned from watching the sport is that it's not always the person who runs down the field in a straight line who scores the goal. You need to go backwards, pass to the right and left, use an unexpected header, and kick from midfield... you cannot stop every time you kick the ball out or lose possession. You have to quickly regain possession and get the ball down field any way you can. Sometimes, you move backwards or sideways to get ahead. New competitors, new laws, and money—everything seems to be an obstacle. Set goals, take risks, and keep moving forward. Success is not a straight line!

Woman with Guts: Kim Locker, restaurateur

In our "Influencer of the Month" blog series, **GRACEDBYGRIT** highlighted local women of note as we loved to celebrate others' achievements. We would like to introduce you to Kim Locker, one of the amazing women we featured, because her story is so gutsy. Here she is in her own words.

> *I decided to start a restaurant when my youngest was born. I also had two young boys at home. Everyone thought I was crazy, but I was not afraid to fail.*
>
> *I will never forget working on the start-up details with my family. I was nursing an infant and racking up several sleepless nights. My brother, Chad, was flying back to the East Coast to meet with lobster suppliers as I renovated restaurant space on the Encinitas coast. My husband, Joel, was negotiating prices for shipping contracts, and my mom, Debbie, was getting us set up as our CFA. When we had our soft opening, I was blurry eyed and delirious, but ready to see if our risk would have any reward. I sometimes pinch myself that, although I had no restaurant experience, I now own two locations. Lobster West has been named "One of the Best Seafood Restaurants in CA!"*

On a personal level, I had to be gutsy when my youngest son, Luke, was diagnosed with autism. I will never forget my heart sinking and my eyes welling up with tears the moment the doctors told us his diagnosis. The fear and sadness I had leaving the doctor's office seemed insurmountable. But then I went into action mode, immersing myself in education and an aggressive plan for early intervention. I changed my priority from running a business to being my child's advocate.

Sometimes "gutsy" isn't about being a fighter. Sometimes it's about acceptance. Over time, my focus on my son has shifted, and instead of wanting to "fix" Luke, or worry about doing enough therapy so he could test off the spectrum, I now am choosing to focus on the beauty he has brought to our lives and family. I am choosing to focus on what Luke can do, instead of what he cannot. Luke makes me slow down, and seeing life through his eyes gives me a glimpse of an awe-filled version of a world that may otherwise pass me by.

Reflections on Guts

Let this be your GRITBOOK that documents your new "adventure." It will be a place where you can write down your ideas as inspiration strikes, but it will also be a tool for self-reflection.

Use the space below to jot down your thoughts on Guts. We want you to think about events in your life that, looking back, showed you have the guts necessary to succeed. These examples probably won't have anything to do with starting a business, but it's important to recognize that your life experience—whatever it may be—counts and can be drawn upon to help you begin something new.

1. **The hardest thing/s I have ever done in my entire life was/were ...**

2. **I followed my gut instinct that time I ...**

3.   Despite failing, I told myself, "I WILL do it," when I …

GRACE

CHAPTER 2

Giving

From small gestures, such as giving up a seat on a crowded train to someone who needs it, to the grand gesture of donating $1000 to a cause close to your heart, giving makes us feel good. One research study gave a number of people $5 each. The first group got to keep the money and the second group was told to give it away.[5] Guess which group registered a greater level of happiness—yep, the givers. In 2016, people in the United States spent an average of $935 buying holiday gifts[6], so, without doubt, people get joy from giving.

Generosity is one of humanity's best traits, but without the gritty moments in life, it may not exist at all. Whenever we perceive a need, generosity is an automatic response for many of us. The spirit of giving is something like a pyrophyte, a plant that thrives when the earth has been scorched by fire—it provides the first green shoots of recovery.

At every level, giving is the positivity we naturally exude to counterbalance the negativity in the world.

Green shoots of generosity spring up when horrible happens. These moments of salvation are truly memorable. Kimberly lived in New

---

[5]   https://greatergood.berkeley.edu/article/item/how_to_make_giving_feel_good
[6]   https://www.investopedia.com/financial-edge/1112/average-cost-of-an-american-christmas.aspx

York City during 9/11. It was a terrible and tragic time for our country, but what was remarkable was the generosity, kindness, and willingness to help others immediately after the terror attack. Giving and love were rampant in the city.

On a more personal level, we experience this from our friends. Kimberly was widowed in her early thirties—an awful thing for a young woman to experience, but it was softened by kindness. While her late husband was trying every experimental medical treatment under the sun, her good friend Priscilla Dunbar (who lived Northern California) would drive down to Southern California, where Kimberly was living, once a month without fail for three or four days to help with life's mundane chores. She would do all the laundry, clean the house, make meals, run errands, and act as chauffeur. When she returned to home, she would call daily to check how Kimberly was doing and provide inspiration and strength. It was remarkable to see and feel. After Kimberly's husband died, Priscilla flew down, moved in, helped organize the funeral, clean the garage, write thank-you cards, and everything else Kimberly needed to get her life in place so that she could begin the process of recovery.

Kate's big challenge was becoming a mom very young. However, this challenge was made much easier because she received incredible support from her family, in particular her mother-in-law at the time, Claire, otherwise known as Gigi.

Gigi gave Kate her support wholeheartedly because she understood her plight firsthand. She had become a mom herself at the tender age of fifteen. The help she gave, from watching Kate's daughter to bringing meals to her because she was working so hard, was generous enough, but it was even more mind-blowing because Gigi had her own challenges in dealing with multiple sclerosis. On some days, taking a flight of stairs can be like climbing Mt. Everest, yet Gigi was supporting and encouraging and helped Kate take care of her baby girl.

We expect you now recall an act of kindness that made a difference in your life, too. These acts are everywhere, though they are too often eclipsed in the daily news by the doom and gloom of the world. We hear stories of heroism and generosity that emerge from the ruins of a disaster—tales of the fundraisers, the volunteers, and the campaigners for change. We are awed by the human spirit and inspired by our fundamental desire to help make the world a better place.

When we created **GRACEDBYGRIT**, we knew that giving would be central to our business, and we believe it should be the beating heart of whatever endeavor you are dreaming of. This may be a counterintuitive concept to some of you who are thinking about setting up a business. Shouldn't running a business be all about *getting*? How will my business even survive, let alone thrive, if I'm giving away my profit? Of course, your bottom line is essential, and we do not advocate working at a net loss so that you can honor your commitment to giving! However, there is a strong case for having a giving ethos at the core of your company from the beginning, and there are easy ways to do it without jeopardizing the enterprise from the outset.

You can see this giving ethos in highly successful companies such as TOMS, with its "One for One" program that gives a pair of shoes to a person in need for every pair bought by customers. Warby Parker has taken the same approach with its "Buy a Pair, Give a Pair" program by giving a pair of spectacles to someone in need—so far, the company has given away more than three million pairs of glasses. Both are part of the current trend of mission-driven, for-profit companies that resonate more and more with the public, who are growing increasingly tired of capitalism devoid of compassion.

The Inbuilt Generosity of the Startup

You don't have to implement the buy-one-give-one model used by TOMS or Warby Parker for your business in order to feel good about what you're giving back to society. It's good to remember that there's a kind of generosity built into the very act of setting up a small business.

The investment that new business owners put into simply existing can be substantial. Jumping through legal hoops, renting an office space, designing the product, buying the raw materials for inventory, marketing the business—everything costs the owner money before any revenue is earned. When an independent store or cafe opens in your neighborhood, the owner has risked a great deal to get it off the ground. They saw a gap in the community and put their own time, energy, and money into filling it, with the hope that risk pays off. At a very fundamental level, this is the first step of giving. A good local business enhances life for residents of that community. The benefits that business brings are social, economic, or both. Small businesses are the lifeblood of our communities, and you can feel good about the fact that just setting up a business is "giving back." You are creating jobs, and providing a destination where people can connect. But why not take it further? Why not get a motivational bonus on top of your regular paycheck?

Build in Generosity

Running a business can be incredibly stressful. The giving aspects of your business might, at certain points, be enough to sustain you through those gritty moments every entrepreneur faces. It may also be the thing that keeps your employees engaged with what you do. According to a Gallup Poll in March 2017, 51 percent of Americans described themselves as "unengaged" in their work, while another

16 percent said they were "actively disengaged." This means that 78 percent of people are either indifferent to their work or they actually hate it! Is it any wonder that the United States' position on the global Happiness Index has fallen so rapidly? Maybe fewer people would hate their jobs if companies gave their employees something to feel good about. At **GRACED**BY**GRIT**, each employee is involved with in the act of giving.

If you want to go beyond the intrinsic benefits of setting up a business, there are hundreds of ways to build purposeful generosity into your business plan.

One of the things that we decided was important for **GRACED**BY**GRIT** was to give meaningful career opportunities to women at all stages of their lives. Our employees run the complete age and life experience range. One friend of Kate's, Vivian, called us during the first month we were in business. She had a three-month-old baby on her hip, and the thought of not returning to her full-time job scared her, but the idea of leaving her child scared her more. She wanted to be with her child. She was honest, eager, and kind. She had experience working with young companies and an active interest in fashion, so we designed a job that

allowed her to bring her baby to work and helped her structure her day for ultimate productivity. That opportunity not only gave Vivian self-confidence but also helped her maintain her sense of self-worth by contributing to her family. With an understanding employer who was willing to give her a chance, she was able to keep herself in the workforce without compromising her ability to parent. None of us will forget the joy of her daughter's first crawl or first step. By giving Vivian the opportunity to work at the office with a new baby, we were all given the gift of watching her beautiful child blossom into an adorable toddler.

We are often contacted by young women (and their parents!) who want to work with us to learn skills and join the team as interns. Internships are a great way to give back, and you get something in return—a fresh look at an old problem or way of doing something. New, quick, and eager young minds can approach problems in a whole different way. Internship programs should never be about indentured servitude! They should be about helping the intern develop professionally. To do this successfully, it takes time and energy on the part of the business owner and company. Great internship programs are mutually beneficial to the intern *and* the enterprise.

One intern came to us in San Diego all the way from New Jersey. Sarah Andersen was going through a gritty moment because her fiancé had shocked her with a sudden end to the engagement. She had planned the rest of her life with this man, so she was bereft. Instead of wallowing in her pain and getting depressed, she found a way to have a new experience in a new place to move on with her life. She thought about what she really wanted to learn and do, and had been following us on social media, so she called us. "May I work for you?" she asked. "I'll work for free. I am a life coach and work with teen girls. I understand them; I know how they think. I also love people. I need a job where I interact with smart, strong women." We said yes. A few months into her internship, we told her, "Okay, we feel guilty.

You're so good, we have to pay you." That was four years ago, and she's still a member of our team. She morphed from intern to having a significant role in developing our number-one social mission with the responsibility for designing a part of our business that has become one of our most important: **GRITTY**GIRLS. Our **GRITTY**GIRLS program (now known as the **GRACED**BY**GRIT** Foundation) teaches young girls that grit is essential, and they should embrace those awkward moments and use them to build a strong foundation. We will discuss this later in this chapter.

For us, the rewards of giving are seeing these women on our team develop and become professionals who make a real difference. Some of the interns have continued with us. We watch them grow, developing skills and strengths before moving to another organization where they can continue to progress. They were ready for more than we could give them in a startup. That's sometimes hard, but it's also incredibly rewarding to watch these women develop professionally as a result of the opportunities we gave them. This is one way we feel we have succeeded in our business.

FROM FISHING NETS TO GRACEDBYGRIT CAPRIS

How do fishing nets become leggings?

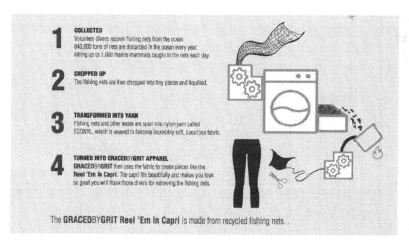

1 COLLECTED
Volunteer divers recover fishing nets from the ocean. 640,000 tons of nets are discarded in the ocean every year, killing up to 1,000 marine mammals caught in the nets each day.

2 CHOPPED UP
The fishing nets are then chopped into tiny pieces and liquified.

3 TRANSFORMED INTO YARN
Fishing nets and other waste are spun into nylon yarn called ECONYL, which is weaved to become incredibly soft, luxurious fabric.

4 TURNED INTO GRACEDBYGRIT APPAREL
GRACEDBYGRIT then uses the fabric to create pieces like the Reel 'Em In Capri. The capri fits beautifully and makes you look so great you will thank those divers for retrieving the fishing nets.

The **GRACED**BY**GRIT** Reel 'Em In Capri is made from recycled fishing nets.

Another key way we "give back" is in the creation of our clothing. We want to make sure that we minimize any harm to the planet. While we sourced most of our fabrics from Italy (we wanted the most luxurious fabric on the market), it was also important to us that at least some of our fabrics were from sustainable sources. We have accomplished that feat. Two of our most popular fabrics are made of upcycled fibers from fishing nets and recycled bottles. They are soft and perform in an incredible way.

We have a small carbon footprint in the US. We manufacture our clothing in four factories in Southern California (we work directly with the women who sew our clothing every week), and we are actively involved in ensuring the highest quality products. We have helped organize our part of the factory, and we can even watch the clothing being created. Once the clothing is complete, we pick it up and conduct a quality control check. Fortunately, our warehouse and store are only an hour from the furthest factory. We believe in supporting the local economy. On a global scale, these decisions were an important part of our story, and it is what feels right to us. Consumers are increasingly demanding local and sustainable products, so this makes sense on an economic and emotional level.

As we have seen with TOMS and Warby Parker, customers feel good about a purchase when there is a giving aspect! And people know when a charitable act by a company has integrity.

Our charitable giving takes several forms:

1. **Product Partnerships.** One of our partners is the Keep A Breast Foundation. The charity was a great fit for us because it is a nonprofit that thinks in out-of-the-box ways to successfully empower young women with breast health education and support. They are innovative thinkers who

support all women, just like we do. It's our privilege to donate to the Foundation with each sale of our Gritty Titty Bra®. Another charity we love to support is the Chelsea's Light Foundation, which was established after the death of Chelsea King, who was killed by a sex offender while she was on a run. This event happened in our community and affected us deeply. We wanted to honor the King family and give back to the cause that inspired us to create active apparel with built-in safety features. We designed the Chelsea Legging®, which has a pattern inspired by the sunflower, Chelsea's favorite flower. Today, $10 from every pair sold goes straight to the Foundation to help them change the lives of children.

2. **A giving option on our website.** One more way that we allow our customers to give is through a drop-down menu on our website at checkout. This allows our customers to give back, either with a flat donation or a percentage, to a specific charity that we partner with.

3. **Employee-led initiatives:** Sherrie Bainer, who was our head of sales, loves to give. One idea she spearheaded was a "random act of kindness" campaign. In the winter, when temperatures in San Diego had fallen to a chilly 40° at night (hey, that's cold for us!), she had everybody gather old clothes and blankets. Then she set up a sandwich assembly table with jars of peanut butter and jelly. One hundred paper bags were then stuffed with sandwiches, chips, and bottled water. The next day, all the women in the office (and some of their children) went downtown to distribute the food. We started at a shelter, passing out clothing, blankets and lunches, then someone had an idea—there were so many people who could not even make it to the shelter, we decided to do a drive and drop with

one driver and one dropper. We visited people who lived on the street and gave away ALL the lunches. People were so appreciative, and we were all so thankful that Sherrie had this idea. We returned to our homes more grateful for what we had and we were thankful for the time to give.

4. **Throwing parties!** Our favorite way to give back is throwing a shopping party. We call them Fit Shops, others call them Trunk Shows. We often partner with charities and causes to run Fit Shops, which is a great way for a group of women who are united by a cause to give back and raise money for something that they believe in. It is also a great way for us to get new customers in our clothes. A true win-win. This last form of giving, however fun and worthwhile, can be time consuming, so here are five key things you need to consider for a successful charity shopping/give-back event.

Time of year. We do events all year long, but November and December are great months to host an event. People are already thinking about the holidays, and the event is a good opportunity to complete their shopping. We try to host the events when our store is closed.

Time of event. Nights have always worked better for us. Establish an event atmosphere by creating a theme. Decorate your venue in a snazzy way—you want your guests to feel like they are attending a special event! Bring in appropriate entertainment and keep engagement high. You may want to go "high end" and glitzy with your theme, or you may want to make it "family and kid friendly."

Invitees. The heart and success of the charity shopping/give-back night is the guest list. Create a list of friends, family, and people who believe in the event. Start early, send an invitation and plenty of reminders. All of our lives are busy—the more you can personalize the reminders, the better likelihood of a great turnout.

Community support. Word of mouth plays a vital role in promoting a charity shopping night. Fortunately, many of the attendees will hear about the event through the charity's members. Give your charity partner electronic and written promotional materials to send out to potential attendees.

Refreshments and nibbles. Always important! Our customers are women, who shop better when they are relaxed. Also, if your event has invited children, refreshments will help occupy them while their parents purchase your products!

But, by far, the most significant way we have always given is via our **GRITTY**GIRLS program (now called the **GRACEDBYGRIT** Foundation):

GRITTYGIRLS

One percent of each purchase on our website goes back to this program. We believe in this program so much that in March 2018 we made it a stand-alone nonprofit and renamed it the **GRACEDBYGRIT** Foundation. That means we can now raise money through donations to provide scholarships for girls that can't afford the program but would benefit tremendously from it. At the core, teaching girls how to cultivate their grit, embrace their imperfections, and feel supported is one of the most satisfying ways we give.

The program works primarily with tweens and teenage girls to help them through their toughest moments in life. Run by our fabulous health and wellness coach, Sarah Andersen (the intern we introduced to you earlier), this program teaches grit and how each young girl can identify the grit within herself: how to get through difficult moments in life; knowing how and when to say no; how to be a good friend; and how to handle certain social situations. Most young girls don't have the tools or self-awareness to develop a "grit mindset," where they see challenges and failures as an opportunity to grow and learn about themselves. Instead, they often avoid failure, are paralyzed by perfection, and base their self-worth solely on their accomplishments. **GRITTY**GIRLS was created to teach them that failure can be an opportunity to build self-confidence, mistakes are vital for personal growth, and our imperfections are often our greatest strengths. Girls learn tools to develop resilience, broaden their perspective, and build true self-esteem. By redefining the way they look at failure, this program gives them an opportunity to explore their weaknesses, fears, and not so pretty "gritty" moments. In the end, GRIT is a part of every girl. Sometimes it takes a tough situation to show us what we are made of. We incorporate movement to develop body strength, patience, and perseverance. We love to give that gift of grit to young girls—it is so critical to their development and the enjoyment of their challenging teenage years. This is not a program that needed to be part of our apparel company; it's a pure passion project, and it gives us so much joy.

Motivation Theory

We can be inspired to start a business by a need to give back to our community or the world. Generosity is one aspect of the "motivation theory" of business, and it's one that appeals to millennials and baby boomers. This is great strategy if millennials work for you or are part of your target market. Since the end of 2015, millennials comprise the largest generation in the workforce, according to the Bureau of Labor Statistics[7]. In our company, we are blessed to have some talented and driven millennials who have taught us so much. They are focused on finding meaning in the work they do. They want to grow as people through their work, which suggests they are searching for purpose. Millennials catch a lot of criticism, sometimes even from us, but we

---

[7] https://www.bls.gov/opub/mlr/2018/article/fun-facts-about-millennials.htm

think their attitude is spot on. We were amazed to learn the following from the ROTH Millennial Survey:

- Millennials mainly connect with products or brands they like through websites, apps, and social media
- 32 percent of millennials prefer to shop online, while 43 percent research online before buying in-store
- 47 percent are willing to purchase apparel online
- 46 percent of millennials belong to a subscription service for purchasing products
- 36 percent of millennials regularly stream a fitness class, or exercise through an app or in-home equipment

According to Paul Zaffaroni, Managing Director of Consumer Investment Banking at ROTH Capital Partners:

Millennials view the world differently and are spending more than other generations. The most promising consumer brands understand these differences and have attracted significant capital from institutional investors.

And David M. King, CFA, Managing Director, Senior Research Analyst at ROTH Capital Partners says:

Millennials seek out experiences and prefer brands that speak to them, versus products that retailers choose to offer them. Winning brands are those that forge authentic connections, market experientially, and exploit the new path to purchase through social media and evolving e-distribution models.[8]

---

8   http://www.businesswire.com/news/home/20171106006270/en/ROTH-Capital-Partners-Releases-2017-2018-Millennial-Survey

In conclusion, use your products and your passion to add to the ways in which you give back to your community. The opportunities are endless. If you have a venue, think about how it can be used by the community. Perhaps you can display work by young, up-and-coming artists at your premises, or offer any unused space for local special interest groups to meet in. Your business can also sponsor a local event, or you can allow employees to spend a few hours a month doing some pro bono work for a local cause. There are any number of ways you can ensure your new business creates a great connection with the community—it's up to you as to what will work best for your business.

A Young Woman that Gives: Willa Thomas

Let us introduce you to Willa. When we met her, we couldn't help but be impressed with her generosity in the face of adversity. Willa proves that there's no better way to show grit than to turn a personal setback into a triumph.

My name is Willa Thomas, and I am a fifteen year old asthmatic swimmer. I live in San Diego, California with my mom, dad, sister, and my two dogs. I started swimming when I was around four years old. Asthma has made swimming challenging, but I couldn't imagine my life without it. It's tough when I have to stop during practice to use my inhaler because I feel like I am letting everyone down, including myself. Overall, it has made me much stronger, because it taught me how to deal with and overcome adversity.

Two years ago, I was hospitalized due to an asthma attack after one of my swim practices. I ended up having to stay the night at Rady Children's Hospital. As I left, I saw all the children's rooms, some of which looked very lived-in. You could tell they had been there for a really long time. On our way to the parking garage, I saw groups of parents walking across the street to the Ronald McDonald House. I felt very fortunate that I had only stayed for one night, and I left with a desire to help other children.

Following my hospital stay, I could not forget the children that were in the hospital for much longer than I was. Seeing them in the pulmonary wing, as well as their parents, who were using the Ronald McDonald House's many resources, definitely inspired me.

I saw how helpful the organization was to everyone and knew I wanted to be a part of it.

I got to thinking about what I could do to help them, and Swim2Breathe was born. I organized a 48-hour swim relay event that took place in August 2017. The event raised $10,000, and in December 2017, we handed over the check to the Ronald McDonald House. It was a great feeling!

Although the Swim2Breathe event is over, I'm still thinking of new ways to support children who have asthma or a pulmonary disease. I might organize an open water swim, or a 5km swim. But whatever I do next, I would love to partner with **GRACEDBYGRIT** *because our stories match so well. Kimberly and Kate sponsored Swim2Breathe by putting the word out and by hosting a shopping event at the store. When I met Kate to talk about sponsorship, I realized I already knew her because she was a coach at my school! It seemed like it was meant to be.*

GRITBOOK Reflections on Giving

It's time to think about your relationship with giving. Of course, we are giving all the time (hopefully) to family, friends, colleagues, and even complete strangers. In fact, we probably give in ways that we take for granted, so now is the time to step back and look at giving more closely and consciously so that you can bring your generosity into your business.

Using the space below (or your own **GRITBOOK**) write about the following:

1. **A time when someone showed me generosity that made a huge impact in my life.**

2. **Something you did for someone else that involved a considerable sacrifice on your part (how did it make you feel?)**

3. List all the good causes you currently give your time and/ or money to and explain why.

4. If you were to build giving in to your new venture, which good cause would you choose and why?

Part II

GRACE

CHAPTER 3

Reason

We cannot tell you what your purpose is. You have to discover that for yourself. It changes over time, perhaps many times over.

Neither of us was born to run **GRACEDBYGRIT**. Kate didn't dream of being a designer of athletic apparel or co-owner of a brand, but she did dream of being a businesswoman when she was a little girl. It's that purpose she feels when she walks into meetings. Kimberly always had businesses as a child: a small theater powered by her younger brother and neighborhood kids, a candy store, rock jewelry, painted rocks, train-flattened pennies, bird cages, and her favorite, a detective agency. She always knew she wanted to work. Early in her career, her passion was science and creating things. Later, it was creating and restructuring businesses. When we began the company, Kimberly had essentially retired. She thought she had done everything she wanted to do, and it was time to focus on hiking and skiing. But that's the thing about purpose—you never know when it's going to strike!

Building our company was the *passion* through which we lived our purpose: to activate the power within each woman.

Sources of Inspiration

Perhaps you're reading this with a nagging anxiety about what you should be doing with your life. We are all so busy dealing with day-to-day curveballs and making ends meet that we rarely consider what we truly want. Additionally, women struggle to think *in terms* of what we want.

We're conditioned to think more about what others want and need from us, and we often worry about being selfish. Well, you can kick that guilt in the butt right now! Living life with purpose is the greatest gift you can give your friends and family. If they see you doing it and doing it well, they'll be inspired to raise their game, too. However, sometimes it takes loss to understand that you can do better and be better.

Kate's grandmother has been sober for over thirty-five years. It wasn't always easy. She was a woman ahead of her time because she valued her career in the 1950s as an interior designer and even carried the weight financially for her family when times were tough. She worked hard, she kept a clean (and beautifully decorated) house, and she drank like a fish to manage her anxiety and stress. But it caught up with her, and she hit rock bottom. Fortunately, her family was there to help her get her the support she needed. She admitted her mistakes, and fought the hard fight to be better, do better, be honest, and realize that she didn't have to be perfect. She learned she had to take care of herself before she could care for others. In doing so, she became a better mother, a better wife, and a better professional. She valued herself, and it was because of her failures that she knew the taste of real success.

Sometimes, it's necessary to go through something difficult and think it's the end of the world. Take Kimberly's eighteen-year-old son, for example. He is a senior in high school. During his sophomore year, he suffered two concussions. It was hard for him to read, focus, and sleep as a result of those injuries. This set him back at school considerably, and he felt as though his life was ruined. Of course, that wasn't the case—his life is only just beginning. He received medical attention and physical therapy for his injuries, started the hard work, and learned how to study again. Whatever the stage in your life and whatever the circumstances, it's never too late or out of your control. Sometimes, it just requires hard work.

Discovering your passion or purpose from a hard knock in life is common, and the impetus for discovering your purpose and pursuing your passion can come from just about any source. Years ago, Kimberly ran a telephone company call center taking listings for the phone book. (Remember those days?) One of the company's best supervisors, who had worked there twenty or thirty years, had a daughter who had cerebral palsy and was confined to a wheelchair. She was the primary breadwinner in the family. She knew that she was committed to a life of balancing work and caring for daughter. She came to work every day happy. She was a hard worker, quick thinker, and an extraordinarily kind woman. With all the responsibility in her life, you would think that she would have been surly, but she went to work every day and worked hard so that she could give her daughter what she needed. One day, she came into work balancing a big grin and anxiety. Finally, Kimberly asked her what was going on.

"I won the lottery," she said.

"What? Literally?"

"Yes!" she said, sharing the substantial amount she had won.

"Then why on earth are you here?"

"It's my job. People count on me. I'll continue to work, but now I know my daughter will be taken care of if anything happens to me."

"Hold on a minute," said Kimberly. "What have you always wanted to do? Call in sick today and think about it. Speak to your husband. You have great retirement benefits. You have the years. I think you should go home right now and figure out what it is you want to do before you come back!"

She did just that. She ended up leaving the call center for good and starting a flower business, which had always been her dream. Now she was able to pursue her passion, knowing she had the safety net of her win to take care of her daughter.

Very few people in the world are lucky enough to win the lottery, but you don't have to. You can start every day by just taking one little step. Each step you take towards your goal helps.

Envisioning Your Legacy

Sometimes, you know you want to do something, you just can't figure out what it is. If you're reading this feeling that you're without a purpose but are desperate to find it, we want to reassure you that you will. But only if you're open to an epiphany! You will not, however, have any epiphanies sitting at home. Getting involved in life, in your community, and in other people's worlds that differ from your own will inspire you.

We found our purpose by chance, by getting involved in the triathlon. And you'll find that our experience is reasonably common. Another example of finding purpose that we love comes from Blake Mycoskie, the man who launched TOMS, a company that combines giving and commerce. Here are some excerpts from the company's website describing the founder:

> *Blake Mycoskie is the Founder and Chief Shoe Giver of TOMS, and the person behind the idea of One for One®, a business model that helps a person in need with every product purchased.*

> *TOMS humble beginnings happened unintentionally. While traveling in Argentina in 2006, Blake witnessed the hardships faced by children growing up without shoes. His solution to the problem was simple, yet revolutionary: to create a for-profit business that was sustainable and not reliant on donations.*

Blake's vision soon turned into the simple business idea that provided the powerful foundation for TOMS.

Before TOMS, Blake, a native of Texas who always had an entrepreneurial spirit, started five businesses. His first was a successful campus laundry service, which he later sold. Between business ventures, Blake competed in the CBS primetime series, The Amazing Race. With his sister, Paige, Blake traveled the world and came within minutes of winning the $1 million grand prize.

Blake is an avid reader and traveler. He is passionate about inspiring young people to help make tomorrow better, encouraging them to include giving in everything they do. His hope is to see a future full of social-minded businesses and consumers.

What does this information tell us?

- He had entrepreneurial zeal, and it took him FIVE times to find his true purpose.

- He saw a need that wasn't being met and created something utterly unique.

- He wasn't driven by profit but by integrity.

- He is always expanding his horizons through travel and literature.

- His vision is uncomplicated: a simple problem needs a simple business solution.

- He is forward-thinking and dedicated to creating a lasting legacy.

Much of Blake's history resonates with us. When Kimberly dissolved her last company, she decided to train and compete in a triathlon because it was an opportunity and new experience, and it would raise money and awareness for a cause that touched her heart. She had just started a new chapter of her life and was not actively looking for a new career. Yet, the seed was planted for a company that would sell over three million dollars in lifetime revenue in the first four years.

We know that if **GRACED**BY**GRIT** ever got to the point that it was no longer making a difference or if it weren't fulfilling our purpose, it would be time to start a new chapter in our lives. We believe that your business should be the best expression of your purpose. If it isn't, you run the risk of taking your business in a direction that does not honor your values and beliefs. You run your business, it doesn't run you.

Family Matters

For many women, their purpose is their family, and we're no different. Both of us are dedicated to the well-being of our partners and children. It's hard to start a business and manage the needs of a young family. It is all about balance. We know firsthand that families—however well-intentioned—can hold you back sometimes, and this is when pursuing your passion or purpose can be stressful.

Our family and friends certainly saw that passion in us, but they didn't necessarily understand it. Kate's father said, "Okay, it is really nice that you're doing this, but what are you going to do to make a living?" Understandably, because she was a single mom chasing the dream rather than a reliable income, her parents were scared for her. But Kate's persistence, hard work, and dedication proved to her family that she was serious, and they couldn't be prouder of her accomplishments or the example she has provided for her daughters.

The support from our families has been key to getting our venture off the ground, and we advise you to get your nearest and dearest on your side as early as possible to give yourself the best chance of success. You're going to need them, and not just for moral support. Our kids have helped in the business—Kimberly's son has taken photos and her daughter has modeled and helped with inventory and sewing labels. Kate's daughters have modeled and worked in the store. For the most part, all four of them do it willingly, but whenever they get angry with us, the first thing that they do is complain that **GRACEDBYGRIT** takes our time away from them. In those moments (and we're sure you'll encounter them too), you get a full punch in the gut because you know that setting up a business diverts time, energy, and thought away from your family. We don't always get the balance right, because guess what? We're human!

The reality is that a new business becomes your new baby. Just like any new member of the family, the pre-existing members must learn to live with it. There was one occasion when the two of us were on a conference call. The beauty of conference calls is that you can do them anywhere. Kimberly was at home preparing dinner and Kate was at home having lice picked out of her hair. (Having kids in school means they can bring all kinds of things home!) Sometimes life and business are indistinguishable. They coexist. You have to make them work together. Believe us when we say that you'll need your family to pursue your dream, but you'll need their love and support even more if you ever have to walk away from it for any reason.

However, if you're not careful, your purpose can also interfere with your marriage or long-term relationship. Much has been written about the stress that spouses/partners experience with a tunnel-visioned entrepreneur who may not fully appreciate how scary it can be to have the family's financial security hanging by a thread. This stress is potentially disastrous. Spouses/partners are an essential (and sometimes only) source of support and encouragement. Relationships also fail because the time spent focusing on the business can put significant strain on the union.

Done right, a new business can bring a family together and strengthen its bonds, but this won't happen if you give your spouse/partner the impression that you love your work more than you love him or her. This topic is big, so do yourself a favor and check out the resources available on it before you dive into an enterprise. Here's one we've found: *For Better or For Work: A Survival Guide for Entrepreneurs and Their Families* by Meg Hirshberg.

There may be people in your life who just won't get behind you. What do you do when they say, "This is crazy! What the heck are you doing?" First, don't let the naysayers (family members, friends, or skeptical investors) derail your purpose. Self-doubts will inevitably creep in when you encounter resistance, but that's when your grit has to really dig its heels in.

To help when times get tough, here are our tips for dealing with the party poopers who mean the most to you:

1. **Ask them to tell you exactly what concerns them and listen** to what they say without interrupting or responding. They may have some valid points you need to consider, but their reservations about your project will likely say more about them than about your enterprise.

2. **Take their feedback and think about it**. Put any resentment you have about their opinions to the side while you consider how their worries fit with what you know about them. If they are worried about your money situation, might it be because they grew up around scarcity?

Sometimes, concerns will be rooted in jealousy towards you, or a lack of self-esteem, or their own fears. Even if you cannot corroborate your assumptions about what's behind their resistance, you can devise ways to try easing their anxiety.

3. **Respond to their concerns**, perhaps in writing or over coffee, by showing an understanding of their points of view. (But don't reveal any armchair psychology--they almost certainly won't appreciate that!). Simply tell them you hear their concerns, value their feedback, and respond with a simple, reassuring message.

4. Finally, if possible, **find a feasible way to involve them in the enterprise**. When they begin to see their input is important to you, their resistance will (hopefully) wane. You may not convert them wholeheartedly to your cause, but you may succeed in getting their blessing.

5. **Use these resistors as practice**! You will encounter many cynics on your journey, and you will probably spend a great deal of time and energy trying to win them over. These family members will help you hone your powers of persuasion so that you can use on the other people you'll need to influence in the future.

A Woman with Purpose: Aurora Colello, Challenge Coordinator of the MS Fitness Challenge

Kimberly met Aurora while standing on the sidelines of their children's soccer game. Aurora told Kimberly that she was forming a team to compete in a triathlon in memory of Chelsea King (who was to become one of the inspirations for **GRACED**BY**GRIT**). As we learned Aurora's story, we became utterly inspired by her and her story of grit and determination.

When a doctor told Aurora she had multiple sclerosis and that it was an incurable and progressive disease, she was not defeated. Instead, this devastating prognosis gave Aurora a new purpose in life. Here are some excerpts of her story taken from her website.

> *I decided that I would register for my first triathlon while I could before my body started falling apart like my doctors were telling me. I had to train for nine months to get ready. I did not have a gym membership, I could not run a mile, and I did not bike or swim. I had always thought that I was healthy because I was skinny, but that is so false!*
>
> *Over the next few months, instead of getting sicker and weaker, as my doctors said I would, I was getting stronger and healthier! Changing my lifestyle and adding fitness (the triathlon) into the mix helped me to fight and stop the progression of this disease.*
>
> *I have raced over twenty triathlons. At my first Half Ironman at Dana Point in October 2012, I placed fifth in my age group. These races have played a huge role in helping me get healthier and stronger, both physically and mentally. Many people with MS are afraid to work out. I don't blame them. We are told that physical activity can*

increase our body temperature, which can aggravate symptoms. I remember being afraid when I went on my first run.

But fitness is something that MS patients should try, whether it's yoga, running or triathlons. I believe that there is a lot people can do to stop the progression of MS. Instead of looking at your diagnosis as MS, look at it as an imbalance in your body and approach it as such.

Don't give up, and don't give in. Every time I race, I think about my MS. I think about all of the people I have met over the years who can't walk well, who are in pain and in wheelchairs. I race for the ones that can't. Anything is possible. I am proof of that.

Read Aurora's story more fully at:https://www.shape.com/lifestyle/ mind-and-body/fitness-saved-my-life-ms-patient-elite-triathlete

To find out more about the MS Fitness Challenge, visit: www.msfitnesschallenge.com

GRITBOOK Reflections on Reason

This fun activity might help you find your purpose. In the space below, or in your own **GRIT**BOOK, try writing your "dream biography." Think back to the Blake Mycoskie bio earlier in the chapter and then consider your own life. What would you like your biography on your company's website to contain? What achievements do you want it to cite? Even if you don't know what business or nonprofit you want to set up, your dream biography will set a clear intention, one that you can use to guide you on your quest to find the best business idea for your purpose. Be imaginative and dream big. Nobody need ever see what you write, so feel free to blow your own trumpet loud and proud!

GRACE

Chapter 4

Resilience

It never ceases to amaze us what human beings can endure when it's required of them. We are often faced with little gritty moments and big gritty moments. We have all experienced some level of trauma or hardship, and, at the time, we miraculously muster the wherewithal to make it through. But it is when that moment has ended that resilience kicks in—that's when we hope to find enough strength left in reserve to recover and bounce back. That's when we put our grit to the test.

At thirty years old, Kimberly had to face one of the grittiest moments in her life. Her young husband lost his battle with cancer. They were only twenty-five when he was diagnosed. For five years, they operated in survival mode. To pay for his experimental medical care, they maxed out credit cards and remortgaged their house. Kimberly stayed in a job she wasn't passionate about, but which gave her the flexibility to care for her ill husband. She took those years one day at a time, one hour at a time, using her gutsiness to carry on for as long as necessary. But then, at thirty, she was a widow in a job she did not love. She had no husband, no money, and no future. The only things she had plenty of were debt, fear, and grief.

Her rollerblades saved her. Each day she put them on and bladed for hours, trying to develop a plan for the future. She knew she needed a drastic change—a life pivot; Something fresh and new. She needed to learn and wanted excitement. She also had to get out of debt. As she bladed, she thought about what she had always wanted to do like travel, learn a new language, leave the country, and operate a start-up. Then, as her legs wobbled from the cumulative days of skating, it came to her. The phone company Kimberly worked for was privatizing South American telephone companies, so she went to headquarters and convinced them that she should be part of the team that was headed to Venezuela. Luckily for her, they approved the idea. The openness to new opportunities and an unwillingness to stay stuck— that's resilience.

Opportunity lies in our ability to not let a situation overwhelm us. We need to mine that hidden source of strength hidden in all of us and live day to day, hour to hour, and minute to minute. We need to assess a situation, step back, and figure out what we can do to create the life we want. Many of us don't even realize that ability to fight is within us, but it is how we are wired. We are designed for survival. We can face our fears, deal with our problems, and create a plan for moving forward. For Kimberly, there was a period of grief, but then, bit by bit, she created a plan for getting back on her feet. She focused on what she wanted—to learn a new language and live in another country. Then, she found a way to do that. It included plans to get her career back on track, which was key to chipping away at her financial burden. Hard work also helped her through the grief. Within two years, Kimberly was out of debt and flourishing in a job she loved. She was learning Spanish, with some hilarious mistakes, and living a new life. It was not forever, but it was something that helped her take her life in a new direction and solved some of her problems. It was also a step towards **GRACED**BY**GRIT**.

Psychologist Angela Duckworth won a MacArthur Genius Award for her research on grit and wrote a must-read book, *Grit: The Power of*

Passion and Perseverance. She uses the word "perseverance" rather than "resilience," but they are one and the same. In the book, she uses history and science to support her theory that grit is a greater predictor of success than talent or native intelligence. She's studied grit at the University of Pennsylvania Duckworth Character Lab and concluded that focused, and persistent grit can be learned. Anyone can be gritty. She breaks it down to four key items: [1] finding passion, [2] accepting that mistakes and frustration are necessary, [3] looking for ways to make work more meaningful, and [4] the belief that you can do it.

Characteristics of Resilience

Dennis Charney, of the Icahn School of Medicine at Mount Sinai in New York City, and Steven Southwick, of the Yale School of Medicine, spoke to a range of people who coped admirably with highly stressful life experiences, such as war and natural disasters. Their research revealed ten elements of resilience:

1. Facing fear
2. Having a moral compass
3. Drawing on faith
4. Using social support
5. Having good role models
6. Being physically fit
7. Making sure your brain is challenged
8. Having "cognitive and emotional flexibility"
9. Having "meaning, purpose, and growth" in life
10. "Realistic" optimism [9]

---

[9] https://www.inc.com/jessica-stillman/you-can-train-yourself-to-have-more-grit.html

Here's why we love this approach:

1. Facing fear is sometimes the hardest thing to do, but accomplishing something in the face of fear is the most satisfying achievement;

2. If you have a strong moral compass, it helps prevent you from making some bad choices;

3. Faith in yourself, or something greater than yourself, will get you through almost anything;

4. Social support is something that we are super proud of in our company. We have created an engaged community of women who encourage one another through both the toughest times and life's joys;

5. We both have great familial and professional role models;

6. And, of course, physical fitness is critical. That's why we started our company. Getting active helps you get through the tough stuff. You need the strength and clear head that you get through exercise. You can't forget to exercise or challenge your brain. Both make life more interesting.

7. Flexibility is critical in any business. You never know when you need to make a vital pivot, and you need to be comfortable doing it.

8. Lastly, meaning and purpose are so very important. We each have it with our families. But it is also important in our professional lives. Showing our children that we have purpose and that we will work hard to achieve our dreams is a key part of what we want to teach them. The purpose and growth we demonstrate in our business helps the purpose, meaning, and growth we want for our families.

Resilience is a fundamental component of grit. It gives you the determination to carry on against the odds, and it is also essential to the concept of grace. By the time you are required to show resilience, you've already been dealt a body blow by life, which is often a humbling experience. Through resilience, we are restored. Better still, we are elevated to a higher plane of being—to a place of grace. Some people are more naturally resilient than others, but we believe you can bolster whatever resilience you were born with, however meager! To unlock your untapped resilience, you just need to be given the "magic" keys.

Key 1: Social Capital

Our social capital consists of our network of friends and family. We saw that when we started this business. Kimberly's husband shared his experience and funding with our company. Kate's mom, sisters, and daughters have worked as models and in the store. Kimberly's son took some of our first photos and her daughter also modeled and helped organize and tag clothing. Our friends have hosted trunk shows and spread the word, near and far. We are blessed. Hopefully, your family is a source of love and support, but if you sense that you're missing some of these strong influences in your life, it's not too late to find them.

Sometimes your "family of choice" (i.e., your closest friends) is made up of the best people to help you through a tough time, whether that's starting a new business or ending an old relationship. Spend time on friendships; never take them for granted. If you neglect those relationships, you won't be in a position to reap the rewards from them when the chips are down. You only get as good as you give, so be there for your friends and family. That's how social capital is built.

Key 2: Self Esteem

Knowing you are capable of surviving and thriving is vital to your resilience. If you don't believe in yourself, one setback could spell the end of your dream. Our opinions of worth are, sadly, vulnerable to circumstances in our early lives, and can be hard to overcome completely. But with some grit, you can work on raising your self-esteem, and this will improve your resilience.

It's beyond the scope of this book to help you work too intensively on your self-worth (there are a million other resources online to help you do this), but here are some ideas to get you thinking about what you can do to feel better about yourself:

- Practice "Yes, but …" whenever something bad happens. "Yes, that bad thing happened, BUT this good thing came out of it," or "BUT this is how it might have been worse."
- Try to visualize the grace that comes from every gritty situation.
- Practice setting doable goals and up the ante bit by bit.
- Don't compare yourself to others … ever.
- Find something you're good at, and then try to become GREAT at it.
- Do something nice for someone every day.
- Make to-do lists and tick at least one item off each day.

Key 3: Sleep

Hmmm … We feel almost hypocritical because we rise most days at 5:30 a.m. so that we can completely focus on work for a few hours before the rest of the world wakes. This is a choice we've made; we're not losing sleep involuntarily. However, if you wander through the aisles at CVS or Walgreens, it's obvious how exhausted America is by the range of sleep aids that are available (the vast quantity of cold & flu medicines, antidepressants, and digestive aids also hint at the major problems our society has with stress). According to a Gallup poll[10] Americans get 6.8 hours of sleep each night; most adults need seven to nine hours. The *quality* of that sleep is just as important as the amount of sleep.

The science of sleep is a growing field of study. Getting enough quality sleep is critical to your ability to deal with and recover from stressful situations, although the irony is that if you're stressed about something, you can't sleep! Then there are also external reasons for sleep deprivation to consider, such as babies or sick children. (We're moms, so we know ALL about that.)

Do you wake feeling rested? If not, you're probably irritable, fuzzy-headed, and/or emotional. These are not good qualities for budding entrepreneurs (or anyone else for that matter). You owe it to your passion and purpose to be at the top of your game, so it's worth finding ways to sleep better. You can try a plethora of science-backed techniques online, or jog down to the library to get Arianna Huffington's book, *The Sleep Revolution.*

We try to get at least seven hours of shut-eye every night, but that sometimes means we are party poopers and often asleep before 10:00 p.m.

Key 4: Distraction

Sometimes the only way to handle stressful situations or forget your own misery is to occupy your mind so intensely that you can't think about them. We love to exercise: hiking, walking, running, swimming,

---

[10] https://www.shape.com/lifestyle/mind-and-body/benefits-of-rem-sleep

a Pilates class ... all of these are great distractions and have the added benefit of helping you sleep at night. Television is okay, in moderation, but find things that make it almost impossible for your mind to wander from. Arts and crafts are great (there's a reason coloring books are so popular now), as is getting involved in group activities where there are lots of people. If you're more introverted, bury your nose in a good book (Kimberly tries to read a book a week and listens to audiobooks while walking the dog and running errands), or take an online course in something that interests you. Just don't let distractions distract you from your goal!

Key 5: Pressure valve

We are both rather fond of screaming! Just ask our kids. And we have both been known to cry (a lot, sometimes). Roaring or bawling are both great (and healthy) ways to let all out all that frustration, anger, disappointment, sadness, loneliness, and fear. The release may be temporary, but it sometimes creates the space you need to carry on toughing it out. Although, as with everything else, moderation is important!

Of course, there are a million other ways—more productive ones, perhaps—to release the pressure build-up. Most of these techniques will be physical, which brings us to our last and most important key of all ...

Key 6: Exercise

Of course, we **GRACEDBYGRIT** girls would say this, but exercise is the ULTIMATE key. Why? Because it can help you do all the above. Sport and adventure travel are great ways to:

- Grow your social networks (Key 1)
- Attain personal goals and improve your body, which will grow your self-esteem (Key 2)

- Ensure you get a good night's sleep and feel energized to face the world the next day (Key 3)

- Take your mind off your problems for a few hours (Key 4).

- Let off steam by pushing your body to its limit, when it is perfectly acceptable to roar with the physical effort! (Key 5).

Yoga might be one of the best ways to build resilience because it requires so much concentration and patience. It also has a ridiculous range of health benefits that can make your body resilient to injury and disease. Kimberly was very resistant to yoga. She didn't like sitting down and wasn't sure she approved of all the chanting and panpipe music that some yoga instructors have playing in the background, but she pushed herself to try it. At first, she just wanted to understand why so many people love the practice. She went almost every day for a month, sometimes twice a day, to give herself a break from work and find out if she could improve at something if she practiced every day. As her practice developed, she began to really appreciate the discipline, health benefits, and the quiet time. Now she's a true convert (though she still hates panpipe music).

Running and walking are the easiest forms of exercise. Grab some shoes and run or walk for twenty minutes. You will feel better! During that time, think about what you want to accomplish later in the day. We love to have walking meetings. They help us focus better. Besides, walking and talking just go together. So, grab a friend and walk! It will help you with your resilience.

A Lesson in Resilience: Zoe Scandalis

We all strive for greatness. What does it mean to be great and how do we become great? These are questions we all ask ourselves, but for Zoe Scandalis, the answer was clear: tennis. Her journey to becoming a professional tennis player has been anything but easy, but she learned to be resilient in her quest. It had been her dream since she grabbed her first tennis racket at three years old. She excelled at the junior level and went on to become a two-time All-American at USC. Here is her story of what happened during her first year on the professional circuit.

> *It did not take long before I was losing more than I was used to. I was losing in a way that led me to become less and less confident every time I took the court. I hit a point when my confidence just shattered. I would look around at the field of players at the tournament sites, and instead of feeling a sense of strength and security in my game, I was praying not to embarrass myself. Hardly a warrior mentality!*
>
> *How can you be great? That is a very difficult question for coaches, parents, and young players to wrap their heads around. There is always a match coming, a tournament to prepare for, a ranking by your name, or an acceptance list that you either make or miss. Most people focus on short-term winning, rather than keeping the long-term in focus: "How can I win next week's match?" rather than "How can I win next year's?" A college coach doesn't look at a freshman and find ways to develop them so that by senior year they are dominating. The coach isn't asked by the athletic director to have a winning team in 2021. Everybody wants wins NOW. Attempting greatness is much harder than one would think. It is HOW you practice that will determine*

your long-term success. I practiced hard and over long hours in college, but I was preparing to play against UCLA players, not the Eastern European player I would face on the professional circuit two years from then.

In my early years of tennis, I didn't go and take the win. I waited until my opponent fell on their face. If you came out to watch USC play a couple of years ago, you'd most likely find me running from sideline to sideline, out-working my opponent. If you came late to the match, it wouldn't be a problem because I'd most likely still be grinding away. In the back of my head, I knew this style wouldn't work at the professional level, but it worked against many college players, and I played for the match right ahead of me. At the next level, I wasn't able to dig out the same victories or find myself in the later rounds of the tournaments like I had in college. By the end of that summer, after almost a full year traveling on the professional circuit, I had a choice to make. I could continue on the same path and hope for a lucky break, make major changes to my strokes and my game, or move on all together.

I wanted to give myself one last shot. I had a serious talk with my old college coach, not only about what I would have to change but how I had to be more optimistic than ever if I were to make those changes. I hit forehands the same way my whole career, and I was willing to go back to the drawing board at twenty-three years old! No one does this. You won't find many players, if any, that have achieved the amount of success I have that are willing to make changes like these. My entire career, I played with a Western grip, which produces extreme amounts of spin. Today, after months of rewiring my brain, I play with an Eastern grip. Just to give you an example, it's going from Rafa Nadal's style of play to Roger Federer's (not that I resemble either of those guys...).

Six months ago, my coach and I practiced with no tennis ball at all. I went back to the most elementary way of learning tennis again. At a kid's very first lesson, they might only hit a couple of balls and do practice swings almost the entire time. After playing the game for twenty years, that is where I had to start again. I had to be patient and disciplined to not skip any steps. I watched my strokes on video every day. After only practice swings, I would drop balls to myself and hit them at the slowest pace just to make sure I was technically right on. Many people questioned what I was doing or they downright made fun of me. My new Eastern grip and the fundamentals I was going back to were very old school. You might see John McEnroe or Chrissie Evert swing a similar way with wood rackets.

"Why would you switch her to an Eastern grip?"

"Are we in the 1960s?"

I heard all those questions and more, but I trusted my coach wholeheartedly. I did feel like a dork some days, but I knew that with sustained diligence, I would get what I wanted. It was simple—I told myself I had to break everything down, do everything right, don't skip a single step, and stay optimistic. As basketball's Kobe Bryant said: "It starts with the aggressiveness and the killer mentality of trying to figure things out by any means necessary and then breaking things down into the most minute details."

For months, my coach and I grinded away at practice trying to solve this puzzle. It forced me to learn about tennis in a new way. I watched YouTube videos of players almost every day and, more importantly, understood the mechanics of strokes in a way I had never thought about before. Fortunately, the perseverance paid off, and now I'm playing great. ,I am beginning to see the hours of work show through in practice sets.

If my goal wasn't to be great,. I wouldn't have taken such a leap. You don't go to those lengths to achieve mediocrity. I define "greatness" as the pursuit of achieving my highest possible level with full commitment and no fear. I'm not there yet. Playing well in practice sets is great, but I want to achieve so much more. But that's okay with me, because when does anything you want badly come easily?

Business Resilience

As entrepreneurs, resilience doesn't just apply to us as individuals; it applies to our businesses too. An enterprise suffers its fair share of lows during the course of its lifetime, many of which occur in the startup phase. It's important to build resilience into the business and its operational plans so that it can recover quickly from any hitches or major catastrophes. This resilience comes from the business owners' problem-solving skills, and the flexibility of the business to adapt to changes in circumstances.

This is a subject that's always close to our hearts. We are open about the challenges we face in our business, and the truth is we are in a new phase of readjustment as we write this book. Just as the course of true love never runs smooth, so the course of your business passion will be bumpy from time to time. Our readjustment came from our failure to find the investment we needed to take our business to the next level, a problem many startups face. Our mistake was chasing after female investors. There are so many successful, athletic, driven women out there, and we wanted one of them to invest and help us grow this business to take on the titans in the industry. We used a woman's crowdfunding platform called Plum Alley to generate excitement for our first retail store and to appeal to women investors across the nation. We indeed met our financial goal, but it was our incredibly supportive friends and family who invested, not new women investors. Two years later, we experimented using a Regulation C (online crowdfunding) campaign. We did see some incredible and talented new female investors who came as a result of articles we posted on LinkedIn. But we still longed for a significant investment from a strategic female investor who wanted to support and grow a company founded and funded by women. We never found one. When we were lamenting about this fact to a male investor he quipped, "Investors invest. Women are not investors." That struck us as absurd. Then, in March 2018, we heard a talk by Sallie Krawcheck (CEO and co-founder of Ellevest). We learned that 71 percent of the wealth that a woman controls remains in the bank.

It's hard to work in a culture that, as a whole, puts you at a disadvantage. There will be plenty of factors outside your control. On the other hand, there is plenty you can do to build resilience into your business.

Our first line of defense for the business—and this is true for all businesses—is the business plan itself. You should always make a plan (it will be required by anyone who is considering loaning or investing money), and it should be complete. Investors will want to be convinced that your business can adapt to market conditions. We'll return to the subject of planning in Chapter 5, but it's important to say that the business plan lays down your vision and your focus. While the way you deliver may change around you, your focus and vision must remain stable. Your business will be more resilient if it has clarity of purpose because it will always have a guiding light that will lead you back to solid ground when you're lost at sea.

The Pivot

That is not to say you should not be flexible. Our vision has remained consistent, but we've had to do plenty of pivoting at **GRACEDBYGRIT**. This is to be expected in any product-based business. We look at everything we do, and we analyze it. We do pre- and post-mortems on styles, decisions and courses of action. When we make mistakes, we correct them.

One of our major errors was following the advice of experts in our field, because we incorrectly assumed they had manufacturing knowledge. We started making our product in China because the experts told us that the quality of manufacturing was better and that, ultimately, the product would be better. We did a fast pivot after we received our first batch of goods (late!) and found a few things were against us from the beginning. For one thing, we didn't speak Chinese or Hindi, and the distance—geographically and culturally—between our manufacturers and us was a practical and psychological problem. We just didn't like the fact that our clothing was going to be made so far from us and we couldn't oversee it every step of the way. Most importantly, it didn't feel environmentally right to ship our fabric from Italy to China, then the goods from China to the United States, and then ship from our store to our delivery firm, and then have the firm deliver to our customer. We wanted our product to be closer to our customers and closer to us. Thankfully, our business could accommodate this change. We now make everything in Southern California.

Sometimes, you create a product that you love, but you are the only one who loves it. We've had that happen. Sometimes, you have to stop making that product because your customers don't love it. We have withdrawn a product from sale because our customers just didn't respond to it. That was hard, because we loved it and had invested a lot in its design and manufacture. But that's the thing with products: it's all about the customer. Our mistake there was not fully testing the product before we went ahead, but in a startup, every decision is a learning opportunity and a chance to make a change.

Startups are all about the pivot; sometimes you must seize the opportunity to change direction. The concept is to reduce the time new businesses spend on research by getting a product to market as soon as possible and then making it better on the fly. Whether this kind of intense pivoting would suit your business is up to you to decide, but we certainly advocate getting started as soon as possible on producing and testing your products. They will almost certainly need several iterations before they are good to go. If you feel in your gut it is time to pivot, work with your colleagues and advisors and do it.

Honest Mistakes

One of our other key mistakes, in retrospect, was our marketing. We simply didn't have the "touch." Rather than invest in marketing, we made the choice to invest in new product to sell at trunk shows and Fit Shops. Face-to-face, our customers loved us. So, we opened a store in our hometown of Solana Beach California in 2015 and tried to replicate the Fit Shop. Our customers and influencers loved it, and it became a gathering place for events and fundraisers, but it diverted our focus from the online customer. We continued to try to market ourselves there, but with little luck.

We had to step back and examine the business as a whole. What we saw was that our e-commerce platform was not as robust as it needed to be, and we had too many inexperienced (but, super smart) women working for us. This led to a difficult six-month journey as we closed sales channels. We rebuilt the website on Shopify, a platform that allowed us more granular information on customers, so we could better market to our core base and discover new customers. But the most difficult part was changing our core team.

Resilient Together

There's an African proverb that goes: "If you want to go fast, go alone. If you want to go far, go together." We couldn't agree more because we know that another important aspect of business resilience is choosing the right partners. It is hard to do everything alone—your business will have a greater chance of survival if your partners have complementary skills. However, it's not just about skills. You need to find people you trust and who you can lean on when times get tough.

We met while personal training (Kimberly was Kate's client), and we continued to train for a few years before we decided to start a business together. We spent time developing our friendship and mutual trust. We took a week and traveled to Kimberly's home in the mountains of Montana to develop our business plan. We knew that working in partnership would enhance our individual resilience as we set up the new business. We wanted to make sure that we shared the same level of dedication, trust, and work ethic.

Our friendship started as a business relationship, and like any relationship, there have been struggles, but we make the effort to work them out. We don't necessarily recommend going into business with your closest friend who you've known for years, because that could really strain a friendship, and the great thing about starting a business with someone you've just recently met is the fresh perspective. Your close friends might share too many things in common with you.

We have twenty years of experience and style that separate our ages, and we balance each other very well in a lot of different aspects of our business. Kimberly had a lot of experience in business; Kate was an athletic trainer. Kate saw what women were wearing and knew what they wanted. We share the same passion for the business and the same eye for quality and design. It's been a great collaboration because we can look out for each other and bounce ideas around together. Our dynamic in business meetings has helped us win backers because we are able to communicate our brand in a way that people enjoy. Crucially, however, we know that if one of us cannot do the work, the other is on hand as backup. Of course, you don't want to do that too often to your business partner because he or she will eventually burn out.

The people you hire to work with you should also be able to adapt to the changes you need to make in the business. Make flexibility a key component of your hiring specifications and job descriptions. In startup mode, adaptation is critical. We made a few mistakes hiring inexpensive and inexperienced labor. Get people into the business who believe in your focus and vision (show them an executive summary of your business plan before the interview), and they will understand the need for swift and sometimes radical shifts in the way the mission is carried out.

A Resilient Woman: Kyra Oliver

Kyra is the kind of woman we always hoped to meet through **GRACED**BY**GRIT**. She stumbled upon our store one day and dropped in to see what we were all about. She was drawn in because she is a keen runner, and as soon as she understood our story and mission, she became a firm friend and advocate. When we got to know her and learned about her, our admiration for her grew even further, and we asked if we might share her powerful story here.

In 2002, Kyra went through something most parents fear the most: the loss of a child. Her four-month-old son, Hayes, had stopped breathing and was rushed to the hospital, but he could not be revived. The cause of her son's passing was Sudden Infant Death Syndrome (SIDS), but when Kyra looked online for further explanation and support, she could find nothing.

In the immediate aftermath of the tragedy, Kyra received an incredible amount of love and support from friends. Rather than gifts of flowers, she requested donations, and in just a few days, she raised about $6,000 dollars. This got her thinking: if there wasn't any useful information online about how to prevent SIDS, she could create something. She says: *"I remember driving down the road and just bursting into the most painful tears imaginable. It hurt so much. It hurt in my body, in my gut, and everywhere. I didn't know how I was going to be able to manage. The foundation and the support from friends and family were just so huge—it was probably the first step toward the realization I wanted not only to help people through my efforts but also encourage them to even do something themselves."*

And so, very soon after the loss of Hayes, Kyra began the Hayes Foundation, which she says was critical to her ability to come back from the devastation. The foundation helped her feel she was doing something to help others, and this helped her deal with her own pain.

But it didn't stop there. In 2006, Kyra launched an awareness raising campaign called This Side Up, which provided parents with an infant onesie that included the phrase "this side up while sleeping" on the front and, on the other side, tips for parents. She found that the onesie was a great way to talk to parents about a really difficult subject. Fifteen years later, it is still enormously gratifying to Kyra to do something to help others. She says that because the grief never ends, the efforts to make a difference and heal must continue.

In addition to the foundation and the campaign, Kyra also turned her attention to her physical condition because she felt that a healthy body would help her pull through: *"One day I realized that 'there's no way I'm going to be able to handle this pain that I will have the rest of my life. There's no way I'm going to be able to handle it and grow from it if I don't take care of myself.' I feel so lucky that I saw this and felt it. I didn't even realize just how amazing it could be at the time, but I did know that I have to take care of myself. I have to be healthy in order to survive this. So, it really started with me walking. When I started walking faster, a friend gave me a pedometer. Then another friend, a business coach, saw that I was having a breakdown one day, and she said, 'You've got to release some endorphins. You've got to start moving.' All of these things just kind of came together, and the next thing you know, I started running. And then I'm running with friends, and they invite me to start training. I really was so naïve to what was going on, but I loved it., I qualified for the Boston (Marathon) as my first marathon. Beautiful things happened with it—the friendships, the comradery, my health. I became just stronger and stronger as I discovered this whole different world out there that gave me a great deal of positivity in my life."*

All this positivity led Kyra to realizing her true passion: wellness, and in 2009, the focus of this passion became a new business called Your Own Utopia (YOU), which helps people develop a healthier lifestyle. She explains the message of YOU is that *"It's your utopia, so you've got to find what works for you. Most people are not going to do the crazy endurance sports that I do, and that's not the idea. But if you take care of yourself, you can deal with life. Most people are not going to lose their baby, and I'm glad of that, but it could be something else, from losing a job to depression. I want them to understand that the better you take care of yourself and create your own utopia, the better you'll be able to handle those things."*

All Kyra's efforts to make sense of her painful loss—the foundation, the campaign, exercise, and the new business—have all lead to the publication of two books in honor of Hayes. January 21, 2018, on the date of Hayes' birthday, Kyra released her first book, entitled *Eight Ways of Being: Motivating Yourself to Live Happy and Free Every Day*. Her second book, *Lifestyle That Feels Good: Finding You, Your Own Utopia*, will be released soon. We recommend you buy both books for more inspiration from Kyra. Find out how to purchase them at www.yourownutopia.com or, of course, you can find them on Amazon.

But until you get your hands on those books, Kyra has this to say about being resilient: *"I think it's important that we take the time to envision who we want to be. It's not about what people think of me, although I want them to think good things, but it's more about how I can contribute in this world. We can all contribute by being our best. How can you be your best self? You've got to take care of yourself and work on your mindset. You must recognize what thing sets you off or causes you to feel anger and frustration. See it, recognize it, accept it, and then consciously make a positive change in that moment. We're not perfect, but my definition of 'perfect' is striving to be your best. So, I just encourage that because it's possible for anybody."*

Kyra has amazed us with her generosity of spirit and resilience in the grittiest of circumstances, and we know she will continue to amaze us for many years to come.

GRITBOOK **Reflections on Resilience**

Personal Resilience

Use this opportunity to assess your resilience. As we've discussed, you have your internal source of strength and you have external sources, such as friends and family.

Begin by writing down who you can rely on to support you in your new venture. This is your "inner circle" of go-to folk when times get tough:

1

2

3

4

5

Next, consider who you want to bring into your new venture and why. If it's not a specific individual, think about the qualities you need to find in a partner to complement your own abilities.

1

2

3

4

5

Now, think about your strategies for relieving stress. Write down what you can do to ensure you let off steam, including hobbies (relaxing pastimes) and exercise (active pastimes).

1

2

3

4

5

Business Resilience

Ask yourself the following critical business-resilience questions:

1. Is there a core idea or principle in your business? Has it changed since you started the business (if applicable)?

2. What talent in your business is valuable for your customers?

3. What technology in your business is valuable for your customers?

4. Is there part of your company culture that is unique for your customers?

5. How can you have engaged and valuable communication with your customers?

6. Is there a recurring revenue model that can extend beyond the initial sale?

Part III

GRACE

CHAPTER 5

Action

Grit is attitude. Grit is doing what you say you are going to do. Grit is *action*. Grit is trying and trying again. Anybody can want to do something. Anybody can intend to do something. The proof is in the doing ... and, more importantly, in the trying.

Grit requires action and perseverance. Sometimes, you can only summon the will to carry out the easiest tasks. That's fine. Do those and then take a chip off the big task. Keep chipping away. That is grit. You can work and develop your grit. The grittiest people take action, though not impulsive action (although we too are guilty of that sometimes), and there is method to their madness because there is a plan behind their action. Sometimes, they've calculated the risks and decided it's worth the effort, even if the odds are not in their favor. To paraphrase the famous Tennyson quote about love: It is better to have tried and failed than never to have tried at all. Grit is perseverance. Grit is continuing to work on something until you get it right.

We believe that hard work leads to success. **How you do anything is how you do everything.** So, as much as we can, we try to live by that simple dictum at work, at home, and even with exercise. For example, so many of our customers LOVE yoga—many of our influencers are yoginis. They are strong, athletic and balanced. We kept hearing about the health benefits. Neither of us were into yoga, and, as you'll remember from the last chapter, Kimberly was passionately *anti-yoga* ("Namaste? Shamaste!"). It was primarily because of the sweat, and sweaty men in particular. Once, while in a long downward dog, she counted the seconds until the first drop of sweat fell from a man's chest hair. Kimberly realized that she needed to use some of her grit to overcome this yoga obstacle. She went to a class that **GRACED**BY**GRIT** sponsored and one of our influencers was hosting. It was jam-packed. We arrived minutes before the start of class and there was only one mat space available—next to an older man dressed only in swim trunks. Kate laughed. Kimberly decided that she had to look inward and really focus. Fortunately, she didn't know the poses, so concentration was necessary. It was going well, and she was enjoying the practice. But the final move was a departure from traditional yoga—the instructor made everyone link arms and do a pose together. Kimberly had to link arms with the perspiring man next to her. UGH! He must have seen the look in her eyes and apologized for his sweaty body just before her arms joined his. She felt awful, fearing that she had given him a bad impression. After class, she introduced herself and said she was sorry. When he heard her name, he told her that his daughter had just worked the summer as our intern. When Kimberly heard this and told him what a great worker his daughter was, he got teary-eyed. Then we *really* felt bad. Here was this nice guy who loves his daughter and works out. It is not his fault that the body sweats to cool itself down.

Kimberly wondered if her aversion to yoga was about more than the sweat. After giving it some thought, she realized she was not confident in her ability to stretch—she could barely touch her toes. Because one of her mottos is "How you do anything is how you do everything," she decided she needed to put some work into this. Kimberly started with some beginner yoga classes at a local studio and has moved from there. For one year, she made a commitment to do yoga at least three times a week. Some weeks, she did it every day. She was determined to overcome her anti-yoga attitude. Today, it is part of her weekly routine.

How you do anything is how you do everything. This is so powerful. It is what we believe. Without action, **GRACEDBYGRIT** would have only ever been a pipedream.

Three years after we had the idea for **GRACEDBYGRIT,** we incorporated the company. Creating the business entity was just one action of many, but it was, perhaps, one of the most significant because it put a very public stake in the ground. That action was the first one that turned a concept into a reality. Incorporation announced to the world that YES, we were *really* going to do this.

For the six months before we incorporated, we researched the idea, the product, and the competition. We spent time together to see if we could be good partners through the ups and downs. It was an odd combination of writing the business plan and making clothing samples. We wanted to perfect the fit, test the fabric, and confirm the quality of the product. We wanted to understand the production process. We have a business selling products, not services, and so we needed to take that action. It would determine whether we would set up the business at all. That's the secret to successful action-taking—learning to recognize which actions will be the most valuable to you and focus your energy there. In other words, don't sweat the small stuff.

We found an athletic apparel technical designer and told her what we wanted: compressive, luxurious fabric that feels great, wicks, and makes women look fantastic. And, we wanted UPF 50+. She was excited and said, "Oh my gosh, I found this great fabric from Italy. It does all that and more. It dries fast, and it's really incredible." We had her create a prototype legging. When Kate received the sample, she tried it on and listened to the sound of the fabric. She called Kimberly, super depressed: "The fabric makes a really loud sound, and it feels rough to the touch," she said. "I don't think it's going to work."

She was frustrated. We were heading out for a training run, and the sample was Kimberly's size, medium., so she decided to wear it. It was a particularly long run, and by the end of it, we were all tired. Kate and our training partner complained about their sweaty, heavy pants, but Kim said, "My legs feel great. The fabric on the pants is almost dry!" The compression and quick dry fabric were amazing, and we decided to use it for our product. Actions are trial and error. The result of an action isn't always the one you hoped for, but that's the learning process. Sometimes, the mistakes are going to be what helps you get to the next step. Taking action is critical. So is pivoting when you make a mistake.

We know how tempting it is to stay in planning mode, rather than action mode. Planning is an action in itself, until it becomes an excuse for further inaction. But it's such a wonderful place to be! It's where you get to be the most creative and the most available to your family! Designing things together and creating clothing we liked was a lot of fun, and exploration was a great phase to be in. However, you need an impetus to shift gears from planning to *real* action. For us, it was the incorporation of our business. It meant we were all in. It was GO TIME. We were ready, we were confident; we believed in ourselves and our concept enough to make the leap, and we were fired up. We knew it was now or never. It was time to get the ball rolling and test our products and our business plan.

Once you have pushed over that first domino, the chain reaction of actions begins—there is no going back. One action creates the necessity for a hundred other actions that spring from it, and a momentum builds that you must have the grit to endure, day after day. For startup businesses, momentum never slows. In fact, it accelerates as you continue to add different layers to what you're doing. Daily refocusing and prioritizing is necessary because the situation changes so quickly around you and there is so much to be done. We made our goals large so that we were forced to maintain momentum and be aggressive about meeting our targets.

Look Before You Leap

Before we decided to formally create the company, we did our research. This is something you should do, however small or large your goal. Here are the cardinal rules for conducting due diligence.

1. Know your limits

Define who you are, who you are willing to be as a business owner, and how you want to communicate with the world via your business. As entrepreneurs, your personal brand is key to the success of your professional brand. YOU are your business's best asset, and people will buy into you as much as they buy into your idea.

Know your values. Be sure to always make your decisions with integrity. Do what you say you are going to do.

Are you really able to this? Can you do what is required to make your dreams come true? Values are also about your ability to step up. Before you embark on a new venture, make sure you have the capacity to take the risk, financially, emotionally, physically, and mentally. You must know yourself as well as you can before you start on your entrepreneurial journey.

Limits might also be imposed on you externally. Do you know the local ordinances and licensing laws? Do you know if your business will impinge on anyone else's rights? Do you know the potential professional liability involved? Don't be caught by obstacles and red tape!

2.   Know your market

Do the work in defining your customers. They will be, perhaps, from across the age spectrum and, in our case, be people of all shapes and sizes. Know their hopes and desires. We have identified our key customer. We call her GiGi or GG (Gritty Girl):

> GiGi is 42. She is married and a mother of two. She has a college degree and owns her own home. She is intelligent. She finds a release in being active and makes time for herself. She seeks balance in her life. She has loving, compassionate, supportive friends and family. She is tough; she has grit. She braves whatever life throws at her. She is a risk taker. She doesn't follow the crowd. She eats healthy but occasionally indulges. She is well read and resourceful. She is adventurous. She is a world traveler. She believes that she has the experience to do anything. She knows how to look her best. She has a story. She has experienced hardship and troubled times—it is how she makes it through those times that define her. GiGi is **GRACEDBYGRIT**.

Our brand is about serving women with a certain mindset and particular attitude to life; it's not just about their demographic or generation. Our name, **GRACEDBYGRIT**, is designed to reach these women and appeal to their sense of themselves. We understand these women because we ARE these women.

3.   Know your competitor

Do the work in finding out what your closest rivals are doing … so that you can do it differently. It's unlikely you'll ever do anything totally original because someone will have been there before in some way. It's not what you do; it's the way that you do it.

4.   Know your product

If you're planning to sell something, whether it's a service or a product, know what it is you're offering inside out—every last nut or bolt, stitch or pocket. If it's a service, develop a robust "terms of service" so it is clear to the customer, and to you, how that service will operate. If it's a product, make that prototype and test it until the seams split. If you don't, an investor or customer will catch you out sooner or later.

One Entrepreneur, Many Hats

The reality of setting up a business is that you must be prepared to do a hundred things you have never done before and may never want to do again. You must be prepared to show incredible grit!

In the early days, you'll have a range of functions including everything from janitorial duty to hiring staff. We do everything. We sweep the floor and wash the windows. We sew the curtains for the dressing room. We call on customers. We design the office. We draw up the contracts. We pay the bills. We make the coffee. Presentations, business plans, and spreadsheets—we hate them, but we do them. Sometimes, you feel like you would rather eat glass but you must knuckle down and do it. You know what you need to do. So, do it. Make it happen. You have to do the big things, even if it means breaking them down into tiny tasks that can be accomplished. Even if it means asking for help. That's a major lesson in life: You must push through tough moments if you want to be on the other side of them.

Of course, there were things we REALLY couldn't do for ourselves. But it was important to fill the gaps in our abilities with the best people for the job. Don't scrimp on that! Get the people who can make your dream happen. We brought in a designer who was the best pattern maker in San Diego. We found people to complete administrative tasks. We also found someone to organize us. We also had all kinds of free help, from people who were enthusiastic about a new business. Sometimes, it's amazing what people will do for you.

We went to an outdoor conference and met a sales representative for one of our competitors. After we explained our business, he wanted to introduce us to his brother. "He sells paddle boards, and I think you guys have a lot of overlap in your businesses," he informed us. We met his brother and he ended up helping us in so many ways. He was there for us the night we got our jeep and trailer wrapped with our branding; he drove with us at midnight to pick it up. (It's pretty cool, right?)

He stayed up late and helped us review verbiage the night we launched our website. Not because he was a stakeholder in the business, but because he was just a super nice guy who wanted to see us succeed. His girlfriend/partner is now also involved in our business. She does quite a bit of modeling for us because she's a local Fit for Mom instructor, and both are now vocal supporters of our business.

That's been a lesson for us: the recognition that there are so many people willing to help you get to the next level when your passion for something shines through. We have always tried to show a great appreciation for those who have helped us, which adds to the fun of our business. So many people want you to succeed that it's not worthwhile jealously guarding your idea and keeping your thoughts and plans to yourself. Share them and say, "This is what I'm doing, and I could really use help with this."

However, be warned: Not all the help we received led us in the right direction. We learned that lesson early on. Every person we sought advice from said we should manufacture in China, so we did our first manufacturing round there. It was a mistake that ended up preventing us from getting our product out for about a year (because it was a full-year production cycle of design, development, and receipt of goods).

This mistake is an example of how we broke the cardinal rules of due diligence, which we outlined earlier in this chapter. We did not know our industry, our product, process, or values enough to say no to that idea initially. Our gut told us that we should manufacture here in the United States, and, as we have gone forward, we have learned to trust our gut more when we make decisions and take action. Sometimes we're wrong, but we would say most of the time we are right when we listen to our gut.

A Woman That Takes Action: Sherrie Bainer

Nobody should be held back by the voices in their head or the voices of those around them. We all have "limiting beliefs," but we cannot let them hold us hostage to inaction. Too many people grow up thinking they're not capable or don't have the resources to succeed, and the community around them can reinforce this feeling of inadequacy or hopelessness. One such woman whose wings were never clipped by societal expectation is our dear friend and colleague, Sherrie. Sherrie has been on the journey with us since the beginning—she was our first online customer and first model. She attended our first trunk show before joining us for a few years as we tried to conquer the women's athletic apparel market. Here is her story.

"Do you think you won't get the job because you're a black woman?"

That question had never crossed my mind before my cousin, RoeShawn Black, asked it of me when I was in my twenties. The possibility of race or gender discrimination had never occurred to me because of how I was raised. My gritty and determined teenage mom had me focused on making sure I had all the opportunities she missed. My parents set me up for success. I never let being black, being a woman, or becoming a mom hold me back. Rather, I wore each identity proudly.

I grew up in San Jose, CA, in the early 1980s, and was raised by three parents—my mom, my dad, and my stepfather. We lived in a diverse community, yet there weren't many other black families around us in Silicon Valley. When I transitioned to the corporate world in my late twenties, I was confident and self-assured. I started working for Qualcomm, never thinking "I'm the only woman in the room" or "I'm the only black woman here." Not only was I the only black woman on the global sales team for Qualcomm Internet Services, but I also managed to navigate the landscape of a male-dominated industry without a formal background in engineering.

When my cousin asked, "Do you think you won't get the job because you're a black woman?" I realized I had never thought about potentially losing opportunities because of the color of my skin or my gender. I didn't think I was any less qualified than anybody else who applied, and I didn't see my color as a limitation. I attribute this to the advantages of growing up in a diverse community, where I was exposed to people of different races, backgrounds, and cultures.

I attribute my career success to a few key things. I credit my upbringing, my family, and my mentors who always supported me. My parents are my biggest fans, and I see them living vicariously through me. My mom wishes she could have traveled the world and worked for a big corporation. She worked a blue-collar job to provide for the family, and her sacrifices allowed me to achieve my dreams. I've also had impactful mentors in my career, including Peggy Johnson and Ken May, and I can't recommend finding a mentor strongly enough. The right mentor will spur you into action when you have some doubt about your ability.

Peggy Johnson was a VP for Qualcomm and one of the first women to help me realize you can have a very successful career and be a great wife and mother. I was at a turning point when I started working for Qualcomm at age 27. Recently married, I became pregnant with my son and faced an enormous decision; choosing between continuing my career or becoming a stay at home mom. While I was on maternity leave, I realized how much I enjoyed working. I loved my career. I decided I wanted to go back to work, and Peggy showed me that you don't have to give up one for the other. I still cook dinner for my family almost every single night, and I'm involved with my kids' activities.

If it weren't for my other mentor, Ken, I never would have gone into sales. He was impressed with my outgoing personality, tenacity, and professionalism, and approached me when an opening occurred on his sales team. At first, I was reluctant. I had never considered a career in sales. Ken noted the qualities that he saw in me, and explained why I would be great at sales. He was confident that I would be successful and offered to be my mentor. Never being one to shy away from a new challenge, I made the move and, as Ken expected, I became an outstanding salesperson and a great asset to his team.

I worked at Qualcomm for fifteen years before taking a job with **GRACED**BY**GRIT**, *a startup founded by women, for women. At Qualcomm, l worked on a team that set up the very first mobile application developer lab for the first mobile app store. I was part of history without even knowing it. Now, in working for*

GRACEDBYGRIT, I am again a part of history. I left the corporate world to become Director of Sales for **GRACED**BY**GRIT** *because I believe in the company and its mission. I was* **GRACED**BY**GRIT***'s first online sale, attended their first trunk show, and was the first mom to model their clothes. I knew from the beginning that they were making a difference in women's lives, and I wanted to be a part of it.*

I was immediately inspired when I dove headfirst into my role as Director of Sales for **GRACED**BY**GRIT***, where I created and managed partnerships. I saw firsthand how empowering and supportive women could work together to build a company from the ground up. We worked with other women-owned businesses that chose to support us, and help us grow our mission, even in the face of competing interests. We worked together to ensure our businesses were successful. Whatever the endeavor, there is room for all women to succeed.*

GRITBOOK Reflections on Action

Being inspired by your mission will spur you into action. We are especially inspired by GiGi, our "ideal customer." In your business **GRIT**BOOK or space below, create a character that represents your ideal customer, your GiGi. One individual can inspire it, or it can be an amalgamation of several people you know. You might find you have more than one GiGi, but don't have too many or your message and mission will be too diluted. Write a character study of 500 words maximum for this person and give him/her a name:

When you have finished your character profile, write down why they would come to YOU and YOUR new business (this will be the basis of your value system going forward):

GRACE

Chapter 6

Acceptance

Now we come to one of the components of grit that can be the hardest to achieve. As girls and women with determination to succeed, we all probably set very high standards for ourselves—perhaps impossibly high. Therefore, accepting our own failures and limitations is not something we're naturally excited to do. When we must accept the failures and limitations of others … well, we hate it.

We expect most of you have experienced a time when someone you love or trusted let you down, or a time when you let yourself down, and the situation occupied your mind, for days, or even months. You replayed the incident or sequence of events repeatedly, perhaps in an attempt to work out how it happened, and you imagine the alternative scenarios or resolutions to the problem until you start dreaming about it. Some reflection is good, but it can catch you in a whirlpool that sends you around and around in the same mind game. This will ultimately get you nowhere, and you'll end up dizzy with regret, shame, or anger.

Acceptance is important to our success. We must practice it whenever the opportunity arises. If we don't, we get too distracted. The things we cannot accept, sooner or later, start to get under our skin and eat away at us. When you're pursuing your goals, you will need all the available headspace you can get. Acceptance is critical. Some things will be very hard to swallow, but keep working on it by whatever means necessary, be it therapy, talking to friends or kickboxing—whatever works. You owe it to yourself and your mental health to practice acceptance.

You don't have to like or approve of whatever it is you have to accept. That would be crazy. That would make you nothing more than a doormat that people could walk all over to get to their own goals. Don't think for a second that we are advocating being a pushover!

Acceptance truly means seeing something for what it is, saying "Okay, so that's the way it is," and moving on.

If you have been culpable in a situation, there is usually an extra step of examining how you would do things differently the next time you find yourself in that position. But what is done is done. Over. Finished. Gone. And unless you're a time traveler, we recommend you forgive yourself, or the other person, and move on. Consider it a sunk cost.

In one sense, "accepting" means to receive something, but it should not be mistaken for a passive quality. Being accepting is an active thing—we have to work hard at it. Do it for yourself, not necessarily for others. Do it for the sake of your sanity. Mistakes and missteps are inevitable in life and in business. Every one of us is flawed in some way, and nothing good lasts forever. What goes up must come down, as the saying goes. So, if you are not an accepting person, both life and business will be utterly miserable experiences.

But that said … don't accept everything! When we first started, people would ask us all the time, "Why are you going to compete against lululemon?" Behind that question was the real, unspoken question, "Do two moms have what it takes to rival a fitness giant?" Accepting skepticism and criticism was often difficult, especially when each of us was battling our own startup insecurities and fears. Kate worried that having only worked previously in the nonprofit sector and as a fitness coach was insufficient experience to be able to pull off being an entrepreneur in the athletic apparel space. She had to accept that she had a lot to learn. Fortunately, for Kate, that was an easy thing to accept because there is nothing she loves more than a challenge.

When it comes to your belief in yourself and your passion for your project, never accept defeat before you've even begun to put your idea into action! It is only when things don't work out the way you hoped, and you've tried everything to make them work, that acceptance kicks in.

Acceptance in Adversity

Our acceptance skills were tested early on in our business in a major way. We had a design for a sun cover-up item made of a UPF 50+ fabric that our customers could wear instead of putting on a jacket or a sweater after working out. They just wanted to throw on something over their shoulders. So, we talked to one of our fabric manufacturers, and together we came up with an idea based on many different samples. However, about a month after making it, photographing it, and selling it, we got a letter from a friend of a friend of Kate's claiming that we had stolen her idea. "How dare you base your business on this?" she accused. It was one product, a somewhat insignificant product in our line, but it was a minor accessory that we thought complemented the product line. Soon, we both began to despise it as it represented a negative experience between entrepreneurial women.

We talked to a patent lawyer. We showed him different clothing articles from other apparel retailers that were similar. We did use a similar fabric to the one used by our accuser. The accusation devastated Kate. It was almost like a divorce for her; she lost weight and was not sleeping. It was a hard moment in our business because we realized who our friends really were and whether they supported us. It is still hard for Kate to think about. Ultimately, it was a valuable learning experience—it was an exercise in acceptance.

The situation required a lot of our time. We talked with the woman one-on-one, but she would not accept our account of events, and the entire debacle took away from what we could have been doing for our business. In the end, we had to say, "She feels this way, she will always feel this way, and we can't change that." So, we ultimately stopped producing that item, which was the best outcome for all involved. In our mind, it became cursed, and something we should remove from our business for our own peace of mind.

In business, there will always be circumstances that will be almost entirely out of your control, including:

- Market fluctuations
- New competition
- Problems with your suppliers and vendors
- Changes in the law
- Consumer backlash
- Innovations that make your product or service redundant

In every startup, there will be plenty of trouble ahead, so be prepared to face the music … and dance!

Some say that detachment is essential to acceptance and that we must remove some of the emotional elements from the situation. Well, we prefer the word **compartmentalize**.

It's hard to not feel disappointed when you find people on your team aren't as passionate as you'd hoped they'd be, or they're not doing what they said they'd do. The hardest part about running the business is when there are things out of our control. These are people with their own lives and passions. Then there's the constant anxiety about the business in general. It's always there, looming. It's the 2:00 a.m. wake-up call; it's the stomach flips when trying to enjoy time with your family.

To manage this inevitable anxiety and disappointment, and to accept them into your life, you must practice compartmentalizing. It's the way we've learned to function, even in our personal lives. When we walk into work, we find our passion and focus, and the frustrating argument with our teenager earlier in the morning is put into a separate compartment. Women, perhaps, are not as practiced at this as men, who have been at it in the workplace for many, many more generations.

Find ways to leave your work-life at work and your home-life at home. If you don't, you run the risk of losing focus in both halves of your world. This is easier said than done, and those two worlds often collide. That said, being self-aware is the key to acceptance!

Workout: Exercise in Acceptance

You won't be surprised to learn that we believe your workout is the best way to practice acceptance. Your body has its limits and weaknesses that can sometimes be overcome, but very often you're stuck with them. When there's something you want to be able to do, but your body won't let you, the only recourse is to accept the truth and redefine your goals.

Kimberly is now fifty-seven years old. For the first time in her life, there are things she must accept she'll never try or never be world-class at. Running was something she was super passionate about as a teenager and young adult. She would run everywhere for miles. She ran through the hills of Berkeley in college, and even opted to run home from crew practice. She ran races and ran to clear her head. She even formed a running club with her friend Tony Cross. Twenty years later, she's finally realized running is no longer the best thing for her body. She's had to downgrade herself from runner to casual jogger and accept this new identity.

Kate is definitely more of an extreme athlete. Given the chance, she'll go out and do anything. But as she builds our business and raises a family, she's had to accept she can't go as hard as she once did. There are days, and sometimes even weeks, when she doesn't work out. She has accepted that this is the natural shift that happens as we age, and our families and work take priority at times, but that doesn't mean the thrills of life are gone! She has simply replaced extreme sports with the energy rush and endorphins of the entrepreneurial life. She will still surf a double overhead wave on vacation!

We would never advocate dropping exercise entirely. Building your physical strength and feeling good about your body will aid your ability to accept difficult situations. When you're rundown and stressed, you won't make good business decisions and you won't be as good about accepting your mistakes. Self-care is essential for entrepreneurs. Luckily for us, if we plan correctly, exercise can be part of our work because it's super important for us to attend classes and meet the instructors.

If you can't spend hours running, or take the time out to do a three-week mountain hike, adjust your fitness goals to find something that works with your new business. If you can't challenge yourself to an extreme fitness regime, find the challenges elsewhere, as Kimberly did when she bit the bullet and took up yoga. Perhaps the challenges are simply about adapting:

- Accept that you can only do thirty minutes a day of exercise, not the hour you used to do.

- Accept that you cannot do a headstand like the rest of the yoga class.

- Accept you can only manage a half marathon rather than the full marathon.

- Accept that the activities you love doing will one day be only fond memories.

With the power of acceptance comes true grace and perfect serenity. Many of you will have heard this famous prayer before, but it's profound in its simplicity: "Grant me the serenity to accept the things I cannot change, the courage to change the things I can, and the wisdom to know the difference." *The Serenity Prayer*

A Young Woman with Grace: Kate Hennessey

Kate is one of the reasons we run an internship program. She is the kind of woman we hope to offer opportunities to and, in turn, to benefit from. She was introduced to us by another former intern, Alex Vidaeff, who became a vocal supporter for **GRACED**BY**GRIT** and who ended up joining us full-time for a year and a half. Kate reached out to us to see if we had any more internship roles and we said yes, of course! She told us that her true love for the brand wasn't recognized until she started her internship: "On my first day," she says, "I was given an orientation of the office, the brand, and the mission. Something that really resonated with me was the mission. The fact that this company was celebrating 'gritty moments' was something I loved and admired, as that has also been my life motto."

The reason Kate lives by celebrating her grit is that she lives with cystic fibrosis, a condition that has turned her whole life into one big gritty moment. We asked her to share more about that with us, and here is her story.

> *"Cystic fibrosis has taught me so many invaluable life lessons, and it has shaped my view and outlook on life. I know for certain that I would not be the person I am today without my diagnosis, my gritty moment, and that's something I am thankful for. But acceptance has been one of the hardest parts for me. I still struggle with it to this day. I think acceptance comes in waves, and as I have grown up and had new experiences, acceptance has had to mature with me.*
>
> *To be fully candid, CF was extremely difficult to cope with as I grew up. Throughout my childhood, my parents were my biggest supporters, and they still are today. They are the people I lean on*

for everything, especially my mom. With two older brothers, I am the baby and the only girl. My mother is my best friend and the single person that knows everything about my life. She has been there through everything, and I thank God every day that I was blessed with such an amazing, caring, hilarious best friend for a mom. Having an older brother that also has CF has really helped me as well. We have an amazing relationship, and he is so influential in my life as I deal with this disease. The two of them were my strongest supports all through high school, and they made acceptance a whole lot easier.

One of the biggest moments for me, in terms of acceptance, was starting college. At this point, I had become comfortable living with my disease and being fairly public about it. (My family never tried to hide the fact that my brother and I had cystic fibrosis; in fact, we held a yearly fundraiser, and over the course of eighteen years, we raised more than a million dollars! My parents are my biggest inspiration and the best people I have ever met). When it became time for me to move out of my familiar small town, leave my routine and comfort behind, and start a life on my own, I was nervous. As I packed up for Michigan, I had an additional two suitcases of treatments and medicine, and this was the first time I realized that this was my reality.

As I walked into an unknown place to start again, I felt CF would hold me back and be seen as 'baggage.' I was worried that people wouldn't want to be my friend after finding out the horrors that came with my reality and day-to-day life. This is when I fell back on my acceptance, however. But I walked into my dorm with my head held high, knowing that if I could accept my reality, then my new friends and new life would have to as well. I soon came to find that not a single person cared that I was 'different,' and all of my worries melted away as I made best friends who helped me through.

The friends I made in college are incredible in so many ways. They pick me up when I'm having a bad day, and they stay up with me when I have treatment. They are my second family and I am forever grateful for them. At a recent fundraiser, I was the keynote speaker. My mom asked if I would be comfortable demonstrating my treatments in front of the entire audience. After approaching my friends with the idea, they said they would come with me. On the day of the event, ten of my best friends drove three hours to Ohio with me, watched me speak at the fundraiser, and then drove three hours back to make their 8 a.m. classes. I am still speechless to this day—the love and care that act shows is amazing, and they are my best support system.

I know that I can't handle this disease alone. Without all of these people in my life to lean on and support me, I would crumble under the massive weight. They help carry the burden, and that is more than I could ask for.

Through this experience, I have learned so much about what I value. I have learned not to stress over things you cannot control, and that life has a way of working itself out. At the same time, I have developed a strong, fighter attitude, and I will never give up on anything— whether that's getting my dream job or beating this disease.

I have learned to never back down from a challenge and to learn from your failures: any experience is good experience no matter the outcome. I value every day that I am privileged to live my life on this planet. Nothing is guaranteed or permanent, and it is important to keep that in mind. To me, family and friends are the most important things in life, and cherishing these relationships is vital in the grand scheme of things. I attribute my attitude and outlook on life to my struggles with this disease, as it has shaped my views and reactions to all life events.

What I would say to someone struggling with acceptance is that it's okay, it's normal, and it will get easier. The only way to overcome obstacles is to go through them. The best advice I can give to anyone would be to always see the light at the end of the tunnel. Too many times people get wrapped up in the bad parts of life, and while it's okay to be sad and struggle through them, it's important to see that there is an end, and your only option is to get through it. Surrounding yourself with people who will walk with you, and who may even carry you sometimes, will help as you struggle towards acceptance."

GRITBOOK **Reflections on Acceptance**

In this exercise, we're asking you to reflect on some painful memories or situations. Stay with it—it will be worth it.

On a separate piece of paper (not in this book!), write down an incident that has stayed with you in which you felt like the victim. It might be a betrayal of a friend or family member, or an injustice that affected you at work. This is something that still upsets you to think about. For the last time ever, think about it again now. Play out the entire scenario in your head and then write it all out as if it were still fresh.

Then take that page, or pages, that you've written on this incident on and destroy it/them. Tear the paper into tiny pieces and throw them in the trash. Better yet, add them to the fire pit and watch them go up in smoke. However you decide to (safely) dispose of them, commit to saying goodbye to that incident in your life and whenever a thought of it crosses your mind, to ensure it vanishes in smoke instantly. It's gone and you're moving on!

Do this whenever something happens to you that sticks in your gut. Don't keep it there; get it down on paper and then let it go.

Part IV

GRACE

CHAPTER 7

Courage

Acceptance, the subject of our previous chapter, is a form of courage because it requires mental and emotional strength to deal with difficult situations. Another form of courage involves not only facing your fears but also running toward them.

Someone might be a brave free-climber, able to hang off a sheer rock face by their fingernails and look down into the jaws of certain death below without raising a sweat ... but we guarantee there'll be something else they are afraid of. Nobody is fearless.

Our bet is that at some point in the recent past, you've told yourself at least one of the following:

- I am not strong/smart/brave enough.
- People will laugh at me.
- What if I make a mistake?
- What if I fail?

We all have a voice inside ourselves that cautions us, sometimes daily. That voice can be valuable. After all, it's there to protect us from making decisions that could threaten our lives. But that mechanism was far more useful when, as a species, we had to think about everything we did for the survival of our family and our tribe. These days, there isn't much to threaten our lives, but our cautionary voices are still active—overactive in some cases—and they are dream killers.

Silencing those risk-averse voices and moving towards something scary is one of the most powerful acts of courage. Kimberly discovered this in the aftermath of the loss of her husband, when she decided she needed to do something different and adventurous to take her mind off of his death. That something was to uproot her life and move to Venezuela. She was at a point in life when she wasn't sure what was next. Life had suddenly become an enormous blank canvas, which could have been a very frightening thing, but it was instead an opportunity to do something totally different. She decided that she would try living in another country and be truly on her own; to test her mettle and test what she could do in this situation. In essence, the opportunity was really to test who she was now that she wasn't defined as a wife of a dying musician. Then (as now), Venezuela was a very politically and socially unstable country, but the job was appealing because it was about making the lives of people better through access to the most basic communication tool: the telephone. This was in 1992, and the majority of people did not have landlines or cell-phone service. The job of privatizing a telephone company was chock-full of opportunity, but taking it was a huge risk, especially as a single woman. It was totally different from where she had lived. Kimberly grew up in two small towns; one in Montana and one in California, and life in a major metropolitan city in South America was totally different. Even though she lived in a luxurious building, the water would go off for a week at a time, the power would go out, or she sometimes found herself sheltering in the middle of a hurricane. When there was a significant rainfall, cars would float in the streets because there was no basic public works infrastructure.

However, it was the ever-present risk of violent crime that was the most different aspect of life in Venezuela. A bodyguard was essential. But that wasn't always the comforting thing it would seem to be.

One day, the guard patrolling the outside of the office had too much espresso and became so jittery that his finger slipped on the trigger of his gun and he shot himself in the foot! Kimberly was upstairs when she heard the shot and thought someone was coming for her. A few months later, she narrowly avoided a kidnapping attempt. She was out walking her dog with a friend when, suddenly, a car pulled up beside them. Men jumped out and put a gun to her head. The dog ran back to the house (so much for man's best friend!), but the two-legged friend she was with stepped forward to offer the men his watch. Once they were preoccupied with him, Kimberly very calmly walked away, trying not to draw their attention back to her. Thankfully, after three years on the job, she made it back to the US in one piece and felt stronger for having taken and survived the risk.

In setting up your own business, you will almost certainly be walking towards your fears. You will find yourself outside your comfort zone on a daily basis. Kate feels this most keenly. Before **GRACEDBYGRIT**, she had never walked into business meetings before with people who'd had so much success and at such a high level. But this kind of courage is like a muscle: the more you exercise it, the stronger it gets. Kate feels that she has more than enough confidence to now walk into any meeting, regardless of who it's with. She's not only willing to be outside of her comfort zone, she actually likes it and is energized by it. But that makes her rare among women in business, it appears…

Courage Gap for Women

In 1998, a woman named Sara Blakely cut the feet off a pair of pantyhose in an attempt to find something appropriate and flattering to wear under white slacks. This lightbulb moment led to her investing $5,000 to develop her invention, and in 2012 she was named America's youngest female self-made billionaire by *Forbes* magazine.

As the founder of shapewear company Spanx, Sara Blakely is openly committed to investing at least half of her wealth to helping women through her foundation. We love this quote from Sara: "Since I was a little girl, I have always known I would help women. In my wildest dreams, I never thought I would have started with their butts. As it turns out, that was a great place to start!"

One of her initiatives is the Leg-UP program that supports other women entrepreneurs by featuring their products in the Spanx catalog for free. Of course, we think this is great, not least because we know how hard it is to gain traction as a women-led business. Earlier in the book, we mentioned how few women-founded startups get venture capital compared to those that are man-led, but when we started out, we had no idea HOW hard it was going to be to raise money. With poor statistics like that, it's no wonder there's a courage gap! Courage becomes even more critical when you're working on a slim financial margin of error.

The investment situation was surprising for Kimberly, who had never been in a situation where being a woman wasn't an asset. She had assumed that perhaps women weren't trying hard enough to compete in the startup world, but she discovered with **GRACED**BY**GRIT** that not even women invest in women! Women do not tend to invest that much to begin with, so it seems there is courage gap when it comes to giving out money as well as asking for it! This is a problem for women in business. Asking for money is incredibly hard, and it's no wonder women shy away from it if it's so male dominated. Ultimately, this has been the most difficult challenge we have had.

We must narrow this gender courage gap and then close it.

We know we can do it because we come from a long line of courageous women. If you look at your lineage, we'd be willing to wager you've got some kickass women in your family. They may not have set up a business (because women had even fewer resources for that kind of activity in the past), but they will have stepped up to do some pretty amazing things, things you can draw on to inspire you to take a step forward with your business idea.

Kate's grandmother, Millicent Diamond, was graced by grit. She wasn't a typical 1950s mom at all. She was not a homemaker, she didn't like to cook, and she was not a physically affectionate woman. She was very much an intellectual driven by social and civil issues. She fought hard for the integration of African Americans within her community where she lived, outside of Chicago. She had the ability to bring in a lot of high profile political leaders, one of them being Eleanor Roosevelt, to speak about why it was so important to integrate these communities. She was actively involved in her local government and had she lived in today's world, she probably would have gotten her law degree, been in government or run a large company. Millicent did the best with what she had, and her husband respected that about her and supported her. In fact, he was more of the affectionate, nurturing parent. It's something Kate didn't realize as a child but can appreciate now.

Similarly, the gritty woman in Kimberly's life was underappreciated till later, when it became clear how courageous she was. Kimberly's mom lived in a small town in Montana and married a man, while she was at the University of Montana, who then abandoned her with two small children. In the 1960s, women in Montana couldn't ask for a divorce. So, she would get Kimberly and her brother on the train to Seattle, where they transferred to a sleeper train to San Francisco, where she had heard that her husband might be living. She wanted to track him down, because in the state of California a woman could ask for a divorce. It took quite a few trips with two little kids in tow, but they eventually found him. Kimberly can see now that it took a lot for her mother to leave the comfort of the small town, where she knew everyone, and travel all by herself to California with two young children and start her life anew. While they were in California, her mom also took the opportunity to participate in the civil rights movement happening in San Francisco and Berkeley at the time. That led to Kimberly's mom meeting the man who became her dad—one of the most generous and kind people of all time.

Courage Pep Talk

Only you can help yourself to be courageous; we can't force you to be! But wouldn't it be wonderful to be talked about in years to come by your granddaughters or women who knew you? Acts of courage are memorable, perhaps because everyone who hears a story of courage is touched by a time when their opportunity to be courageous passed them by. Don't let your moment disappear. Grab that opportunity by the horns and hang on, and whether you successfully ride it out or whether you fall off in five seconds, the fact is that you tried. Whoever said that it is better to regret something you did than regret something you didn't do, was a very wise person indeed.

But in case you need some extra words of en*courage*ment, here are some from a selection of truly remarkable people:

**"Success is not final; failure is not fatal:
it is the courage to continue that counts."**

Winston Churchill

"Your time is limited, so don't waste it living someone else's life. Don't be trapped by dogma - which is living with the results of other people's thinking. Don't let the noise of others' opinions drown out your own inner voice. And most important, have the courage to follow your heart and intuition."

Steve Jobs

"There is no living thing that is not afraid when it faces danger. The true courage is in facing danger when you are afraid."

L. Frank Baum, *The Wonderful Wizard of Oz* (published 1900)

"Passion is what drives us crazy, what makes us do extraordinary things, to discover, to challenge ourselves. Passion is and should always be the heart of courage."

Midori Komatsu

"It's not the size of the dog in the fight, it's the size of the fight in the dog."

Mark Twain

"Courage doesn't always roar. Sometimes courage is the little voice at the end of the day that says I'll try again tomorrow."

Mary Anne Radmacher, author of *Courage Does Not Always Roar: Ordinary Woman with Extraordinary Courage.*

"Jump, and you will find out how to unfold your wings as you fall."

Ray Bradbury

"Courage is grace under pressure."

Ernest Hemingway

A Woman with Courage: Courtney Brickner

We've mentioned Courtney previously, but we want to return to her here: she inspires us!

Courtney runs her own business, Brickhouse Fitness, which she began in 2012, and we are delighted she is one of our "influencers." She is such a positive human being, like all the women we work with, however, she has a gritty story, and we think she's very courageous to have confronted and conquered her personal challenge: alcohol addiction. Here is her story.

> *"I was not the type of alcoholic that most people, myself included, visualized. I didn't understand how I could have a problem with drinking when I had no problem holding a job, taking care of my family, and getting everywhere I needed to be on time. But the reality was that I drank every night and blacked out most of the time.*
>
> *I finally realized alcohol was an issue for me when I was thirty-five and starting to have health problems. I developed a chronic cough that bothered me all day, every day. Sometimes, I would wake up at night coughing uncontrollably, unable to catch my breath. I was choking, and unable to breathe. I even coughed so much that I vomited in the bed. I went to the doctor to have it checked out, and she thought it might be acid reflux. She prescribed a medication, but didn't seem to work. I went back about a month later when the cough still had not gone away. She then said it might be allergies and post-nasal drip. She prescribed a nasal spray. Still, the cough did not get better.*
>
> *I looked online at my symptoms to see what else it could be, and found that excessive drinking could cause it. When the doctor*

asked me about my drinking, I told her I had about one drink per day. I lied because I didn't want to tell her that I really had about four or five drinks per day. I also decided not to tell my husband what I had read online because I didn't want him to tell me I should stop drinking. At that point in time I knew I drank too much, but I really didn't want to stop because I liked it so much. However, I also knew that my health was not going to get any better. In fact, it would probably get worse if I continued.

In 2012, my husband and I went on a vacation, like we did every summer, where we pretty much drank every day. It was a typical vacation in every way. However, when we got back home, I couldn't stop thinking about how I had drunk vodka from about 11am-3am for one week straight, but because my tolerance for it had gotten so high, I never really felt a major effect from it. I also realized after we returned home that all I was thinking about was getting through the day until it was "an acceptable" time to start drinking.

I knew that spending my days thinking about drinking, my nights drunk and passed out, and my mornings recovering (all while getting sicker) was not the life I wanted for my children or me. So, on August 18, 2012, I decided that I would stop drinking. The desire was still fully there, but I knew I couldn't go back, so I didn't take another drink.

I didn't do anything special to recover from my addiction at the time except stop drinking. I made some simple changes, like declining invitations to events where I knew everyone would be drinking. I didn't share the fact that I wasn't drinking anymore with too many people because I didn't want to be the "weird" person, so I just made up excuses as to why I couldn't go. If I did happen to be at an event where there was drinking, I just said no thanks. People always assumed it was because I was fit and very concerned with my health. My husband and I had to make some lifestyle changes because we really were drinking buddies. We had to think of other things to do with our time, and I was nervous that we wouldn't be able to do it.

In the beginning, it was tough being sober because there were people who said, "You're not an alcoholic, you just like to have fun." I really wanted to believe them, but I knew it wasn't true. I struggled with even saying the words "I'm an alcoholic" for a VERY long time. After about three years, I didn't feel like it was getting any easier. Even though I hadn't had a drink, I still felt like I wanted to, and still felt pissed off and sad that I couldn't. I thought maybe if I just had one drink now and then that it wouldn't be that big of a deal. But I had tried making rules like that in the past and none of them worked, so I didn't test it out. I decided that going to an AA meeting might be what I needed because I had never ventured down that path since I had been sober.

The first day I went to AA, I was very nervous and didn't feel like I would fit in because I wasn't a "real" alcoholic. Little did I know alcoholics come in all forms. It's not just the person that can't hold a job and is close to being homeless. I felt so at home at the first meeting because the people that spoke were telling my story. I cried and realized that this was where I needed to be. I went five days a week for about a year and learned about how to deal with my emotions, which I wasn't good at before. It was through AA that I realized drinking was not the problem; it was a symptom. I had to get down to what the real issues were, which wasn't fun. I don't go to meetings as frequently now, but the tools I got from going to AA have remained with me, and I use them still.

I still have trouble dealing with emotions sometimes—my first response is to bury things deep inside so I don't have to deal with them. When I was drinking, the alcohol helped numb the feelings that I didn't want to give a voice to. Now, even though I can shut down briefly, I know that I don't have an escape from what I'm dealing with. I have to face it head on and sometimes have difficult conversations. I would say that courage is coming face to face with something that scares, intimidates, or stresses you out, but nonetheless you decide to battle it.

There are occasional days that I think a drink would fix my situation, but I quickly remember what my life was like and figure out another way. I would tell someone dealing with addiction that it can be better. What you are feeling now doesn't have to always be that way. There are tools you can use that work. You can be happy.

Even though people have to get sober for themselves, in my case thinking about the people that I was affecting made all the difference to me. My husband's support has been unwavering and has helped me so much. I think I scared him when I would wake up choking. He wanted me to get better so badly. I knew I had to remain strong for him and my kids. It's important to remember that there are people that need you and care about you, and you need to remember that you are worth it. You don't have to be ashamed. I never wanted to tell anyone, but now I don't really care; I actually prefer that they know because I think it's important that the vision of what an alcoholic is changes.

I got involved with GRACEDBYGRIT's Influencer Program when I heard about the company from a friend. I looked it up, read their mission statement and was so moved. The whole story of the company really spoke to me, and it made me feel that I wouldn't be judged for my gritty situation. I would say to anyone who needs more courage to get through a gritty situation to find your support network—your people— and keep on the path to fulfilling your true potential."

GRITBOOK **Reflections on Courage**

Who do you look up to? Who inspires you with their grit?

Write about this person below or in your journal: who they are, what they do, and why they are so inspirational to you. It can be someone close to you or it can be someone from the world of business or faith. Whoever it is, this is the person you should think about in the low moments. What would this person do in your shoes? Hopefully, this will be enough to spur you on.

GRACE

CHAPTER 8

Character

We are living in an age in which customers no longer like faceless corporations. They like to connect on a personal level with the company, and this is especially true of millennials, who, for many of you, will be your main target market.

But let's get one thing straight: you cannot define your passion until you understand yourself. If you do not have clear insight into your own character, your business will struggle to find its identity. Without an identity, your business will not appeal to customers, and it will ultimately fail. Who you are forms the heart of your enterprise, so it's worth taking the time during your brand planning to ensure your character is taken into consideration. As a startup, this is especially important.

Who *you* are will determine the following (among many other things):

- Which customers will identify with you ... and which customers you want to avoid
- The tone of your social media and your website
- Your sales techniques and pricing
- Who you hire
- What kind of investors you want to pursue

- How your company will grow
- The relationship with your community

Your *identity* is key to your business's *integrity*.

The moment customers suspect you're disingenuous, they will cut you off. Integrity is an important ethic for any entrepreneur, and this feeds into the discussion on ethics in the next chapter.

Company Character

For a great example of how the individual informs the business, look no further than Yvon Chouinard, the founder of the outdoor apparel company Patagonia. An avid rock climber, his eco-warrior persona is the foundation on which the company is built. The focus of Patagonia is human outdoor pursuits but not if your outdoor pursuit involves an engine of any description. Any pollution or endangerment to the environment is a big no-no. Chouinard himself famously encouraged his employees to abandon work and go surfing whenever the swell came in! He also ensured that his company paid a 1% self-imposed "earth tax" on all sales, and the money goes to grassroots environmental groups. In a fascinating 2016 article in *The New Yorker*[11], Chouinard is quoted as saying: "The capitalist ideal is you grow a company and focus on making it as profitable as possible. Then, when you cash out, you become a philanthropist. We believe a company has a responsibility to do that all along—for the sake of the employees, and for the sake of the planet."

What's also interesting about Chouinard is that he hates to be defined as a businessman because he says he has no respect for his profession, but we respect him for having created a company whose brand we

---

[11]   https://www.newyorker.com/magazine/2016/09/19/patagonias-philosopher-king

identify with. Patagonia is true to its brand, true to quality, and true to its customers.

We like to compare ourselves to Patagonia in terms of our character and quality of product. Although, at **GRACEDBYGRIT**, we focus on activating the power within women to become their best selves through exercise, because that is what we did ourselves! (More about this in Chapter 9.) We are more inward focused than Patagonia, which we feel is more about humans vs. nature on a macro scale. We like to operate on a micro scale; it's all about helping individual women in harness that grit, get outside, and get physically fit so they can face the challenges of their lives.

The Startup: The Ultimate Character Test

You may think you know yourself well before you set up a business, but we can guarantee you will learn far more about your character once you've begun the journey. Some of those realizations will be wonderful, others not so much.

Kate learned that she was stronger and smarter than she previously thought, simply because she was suddenly using her brain in a very different way. But the experience also reinforced what she already knew: "Once a coach, always a coach." It turned out that Kate likes to manage people in a similar way to how she coached swimmers and runners: a mix of tough love, encouragement, and fun.

Kate also used to think that her day wasn't complete unless she'd broken a sweat, but mental exercise has become just as stimulating as physical workouts. She has experienced more intellectual challenges over the last four years than ever before. In the process, she has realized that listening to her gut is super important and very reliable.

Kimberly, however, learned that she isn't the tolerant person she thought she was! She's always understood that she can't work with people who make excuses or don't tell the truth. She also discovered a dread of asking people for money, which is unfortunate when the critical part of a startup is asking! Unless you're asking for a donation for a good cause, nobody likes to ask for money. Each time Kimberly thinks, *Oh, God, I've got to go ask them again. What if they say no? What am I going to do next?* When the "no's" come, and they have in droves, just as they do for everyone in a startup, it's hard. Kimberly and Kate are still learning how to accept them and overcome them.

The Gritty Entrepreneur

In the startup world, all sorts of characters can survive and thrive. But they all have one thing in common: grit. They embody, each in their different ways, the characteristics we've been talking about in this book. However, we've defined some more specific qualities that we believe helped us along the way.

Be Decisive

People who are afraid to make a decision will almost certainly fail in business. Even a wrong decision is better than none! Too many people overanalyze things and, in doing so, paralyze themselves and their business. You can't afford to be stuck in a rut or be afraid to make a mistake. Mistakes are an inevitable part of any startup, and sometimes you've got be the one to make a decision. If it turns out to be a bad one, own it. We've made a few of those ourselves, and have learned from them.

Be Focused

You'll realize that there are some things you can no longer do in your life, so you have to pick and choose which are the most important.

Alternatively, find a "life hack"—a workaround technique for managing your life more effectively.

Kimberly is a woman of faith, and before the company took off, she enjoyed participating in a weekly Bible study. The time of the study no longer works for her, but the woman who runs it is kind enough to summarize what was discussed and what everyone felt they learned. She can now participate by just reading the notes sprinkled with occasional visits.

There are hundreds of technology-based hacks that can help you manage your time more efficiently and help you be more focused.

Inevitably, however, when you're running a business, it's hard to maintain the schedule your family and friends were used to before it got in the way. But to succeed, you must be prepared to shift those relationships a bit and focus your time together on *quality* instead of quantity. If they love you and respect what you're trying to do, they'll work with you on redefining the boundaries.

Be a Delegator

When you start something, you'll soon find that everyone wants your time, attention, and validation of their work. They'll also assume that you'll make all the decisions. In our company, Kimberly led the way in empowering our team to make as many decisions as is practical. Of course, there will always be those that we must make and be party to, but it's impossible to be in on every meeting or conversation.

In delegating, be prepared for the occasional wrong decision. As we said earlier, mistakes are unavoidable, so figure out a way to support your decision-makers when things go wrong. The key to good management is not only rewarding employees for their successes but also taking responsibility for their failures. If you're smart about your hiring choices, however, failure will be less of a concern.

We are relentless in both good and negative ways. Relentlessness is important when you start a business. It requires so much dedication and hard work that it's necessary, but it can be hard for team members who don't function with that type of personality. We curated a team of women who are more like us than not. We all have strong personalities and opinions—we are all relentless.

Our team is a group of super-phenomenal women at every stage of their lives. Some are still learning, and it is fun to watch the like-minded talent making the decisions, people who don't need us to hold their hands every step. And this leads us into an important arena: intelligent hiring.

Character Match

One of the best pieces of advice we can give you is to hire people who embody the character of the company you are trying to build. It's tempting to opt for expediency over appropriateness when it comes to hiring—as a startup, you're up against time pressures. But don't do what we did in the beginning, which was to hire a lot of people who were available, who happened to live nearby, or whom we knew well (and perhaps worked with previously). While this helped us get up and running, this approach also led us to poor hiring decisions.

Look for potential AND experience. We all need a break early in our careers, but traditional hiring practices look for previous experience that not everyone who's right for you will have. We have a woman who works for us in customer service, operations, and inventory management, who came to Southern California for a love interest, and now, she's someone who could potentially run this company one day.

We also had a young girl who was a student at the Fashion Institute in Chicago and would call us all the time wanting an internship. We didn't really have room for her, but she was so persistent that we brought her on. She got herself out here, started working, and she's been incredible. She is strong, smart, and she's a risk-taker: we just think she's inspirational!

In that instance, everything worked out. But we soon discovered it was best to be strategic. After feeling around in the dark for a while, we now use a predictive index (PI) tool when we hire. Hiring people is much like online dating. Initially, you have only their word for their character, and figuring out whether he or she is right for you can be difficult. PI is an invaluable human resource tool that consists of a very short assessment that allows you to see how the behaviors in someone's personality would lead to job success. It's not about a candidate being right or wrong, or good or bad; it's purely about identifying that person's character traits so that you can find the right placement for them within the company. As an example, you can't put somebody that has no attention to detail in production when everything is about detail!

We have created profiles—detailed personnel specifications—for all our key jobs. Our hiring process includes a quiz that's tailored to that job. Before an interview is set up, candidates complete the quiz, and their answers show us if they have the personality traits to be able to perform successfully within that job. It's worthwhile building those job profiles when you start out so that you can get the right people from the very beginning. Our customer, friend and neighbor, Mary McGuiness, taught us how to use and interpret the data.

PI is a great resource because it takes the emotion and gut instinct out of hiring and puts everyone on an even playing field. Experience becomes less important than enthusiasm and aptitude. The person-to-person interviews are also easier because you can form the right questions to ask.

Once you understand your team members' different personalities, you can begin to look for people who can fill gaps in your company, and seek those who will work best within the office setting and culture in terms of how they communicate with each other and get the job done.

PI also provides an interesting opportunity for the women we hire to learn about themselves. Often, there's some resistance at the beginning, and employees occasionally say, "No, that's not me." But as time passes, they realize the PI results were correct!

To be an authentic brand, each of our employees must have a character that fits our ethos and mission, but that does NOT mean they are a homogeneous bunch. We are all from different backgrounds and at different stages of life. This is great, because we love to learn from all of the women we work with!

A Woman with Character: Liz Lawson

Kate and Liz met when Kate first moved to San Diego and became a single mom. They became fast friends, and they started running together to talk through work and life. Liz is a natural role model. Other women instinctively look up to her, which is testament to the strength of her character.

> Liz was a volunteer at a Boys and Girls Club aquatics program, where her three kids went swimming, when she met Kate. A retired teacher, Liz is a natural with people. It was probably inevitable Liz would get involved with the Club, but when the task of organizing swim meets became too large, the Club hired a new person: Kate. So, Liz trained her, and the rest is history.
>
> People like Liz are the kind of friend you want in your corner; the kind of friend that has your back. When Kate talked to her about starting a business, Liz was instantly supportive. She offered to host a trunk show at her house. Remembering this, she says, "You know how people have Tupperware parties and things like that at their homes? Well, I don't do that because I don't like those kind of parties, but I thought, 'I like Kate and I like the clothes, so I'll have one at my house!'"
>
> She quickly realized she had bitten off more than she could chew with our fledgling company! We arrived at her house embarrassingly ill-prepared—it was our first time, too! There were no price tags on any of the clothes, and we didn't have a mirror, or even a table to spread out our stuff on. Admittedly, it was a bit of a mess. Liz is never wispy or shy, and told us to up our game, pronto. At the end of the show, we asked her if she

would help us get more organized. "Sure," she said. "I'm good at organizing. I would love to help."

That was almost five years ago. Liz is now our stock manager and an indispensable part of the team.

Liz's key quality is being highly organized. It is not a trait that everyone has by any means (the state of our stock when we first started our business will attest to that fact!). She attributes this quality to having been a teacher for many years. It's her teaching background that makes her the kind of character who is a natural role model. "We look to the people who are just ahead of us in life," Liz says, with her characteristic humility. "You pick out people you think are doing something well, and you want to do it like they did. I've also had people in my life like that."

Kate feels that Liz is a mentor, and she's often reached out to her for parenting advice. There was an occasion when Liz counseled Kate about the necessary changes in parental behaviors over time: what you can get away with around young kids compared to how you need to behave with teenagers. This advice was extremely valuable to Kate, and she took it to heart. That kind of role modeling is not about "knowing it all" and being superior; it's simply about having more experience and being unafraid to share it. Liz says, "I think it comes easily to me. I don't want to sound braggy, like I know what I'm doing because I don't. I'm guessing at life like everyone else is. I've just been through all the things that Kate's going through with her kids growing up. I have three children, and I've dealt with every scenario. It's always great to have a friend who's been through it." We all need friends in our lives like this, and they make great additions to a business team.

Liz fits in perfectly at **GRACED**BY**GRIT**. We know what personality works well with us. If you're aloof, you're not going to do well with our company. Like Liz, you have to be on your game and be able to change hats at a moment's notice. At **GRACED**BY**GRIT**, when a truck shows up with items that need to be unpacked, everybody drops what they're doing, unpacks, then starts sorting.

And what character traits does Liz admire?

"I can't stand people who say they're going to do something, and they don't follow through and do it. I like people who follow through," she says. However, honesty is the most important quality for Liz: "Say it like it is. Be real. If you have a big butt, be like, 'Wow, I have a big butt!' Don't be like, 'No one must ever mention my big butt!'"

That's our kind of woman! Who is yours?

GRITBOOK **Reflections on Character**

Take this opportunity to think about your character in an as objective a way as possible. Again, nobody will read this or your business **GRITBOOK**, so be as brutally honest or as outrageously vain as you like. It doesn't matter that others may see you differently; what matters here is how you see yourself. When you understand yourself this way, you can think about what traits you want to develop further and those which you want to try minimizing or mitigating.

My greatest strengths are …

My biggest flaws are …

Five words that sum me up as a friend …

Five words that sum me up as a spouse/partner …

Five words that sum me up as an employee …

Part V

GRACE

Chapter 9

Empathy & Enjoyment

Empathy

Empathy—the ability to walk (or run, in our case) in other people's shoes and feel what they feel. We believe this is critical to the concept of grace and grit. Once we can see something from someone else's perspective, we can understand how to help them, and overcome any problem we have with that person or situation.

Empathy is not only an essential skill for living; it has become a central pillar of business. Why? Because business is all about relationships, and relationships need understanding to survive.

Sociopaths are people with no empathy, and it's impossible to have lasting and fulfilling relationships with them. The same is true of psychopathic corporations. They will ultimately fail when their aggressive business tactics stop working, and they are no longer considered consumer-friendly. When those companies go through a rebranding exercise, quite often they'll try to put on an empathetic front. We don't like things that are made up, like when brands say that they have a certain story, but they really don't.

GRACEDBY**GRIT** is founded on respect for all body types and a love of listening to women's stories. This motivates us to create our clothing, and to be great at what we do. Whenever we do anything, we ask a bunch of questions:

What does our customer feel?

What does she think?

What's important to her?

What frustrations is she feeling?

How would she like to change it?

It is not a gimmick. It is a genuine desire to help women feel powerful and strong when they are working out and living every part of their lives. It's a desire because we know what it feels like to be those women; we understand each person's story. Almost every time one of our customers comes into the store, they tell us how they have been graced by grit. Those stories, those gritty and graceful moments, are key contributors to how we design our clothes, and they inform our company blog (there are a whole bunch of inspiring stories there, so we hope you subscribe to it sometime!).

But listening is only one part of empathy in business. You must ACT! It won't be enough to nod and say, "We hear you," if nothing changes as a result. Look for ways you can demonstrate your empathy. Here are some examples from our business of the ways we responded to feedback.

- One of our first products, our fleece-lined legging, was developed because one of our employees wanted something that could keep her warm while she was trying to shed some extra weight. We searched and searched until we found a warm fabric that was also flattering so that she felt less self-conscious about her weight.

- Our self-defense classes were developed to address the safety concerns we hear about from our customers. Our clothing already had safety features, but we wanted women to feel more empowered in their bodies to protect themselves.

- We manufacture our clothing in the US in response to demands from our customers, and it fit well with what we wanted to do—their demands gave us the confidence to transition to supporting the domestic economy.

- Similarly, our customers are helping us drive a positive change on our environmental impact. Several clients love our great Italian fabrics, but they worried that buying them was bad for the environment because of the distance from source to production. This made sense, and we now source fabrics from around the world, and have included sustainable fabrics made from recycled water bottles and fishing nets. Sustainability has become a key part of our company, which dovetails with our Southern California factories to reduce our carbon footprint.

- XXS and XXL sizing came from customer feedback.

Your empathy informs your personal ethics. And, if you're considering setting up a business or a nonprofit, it will inform the ethics of your enterprise. Ethics are, in essence, the promises you make to yourself or, in the business context, to your customers (in product-driven businesses) or clients (in service-driven businesses).

Our business ethics are:

EMPOWERMENT: Supporting women to be their best selves through our products

SAFETY: Helping women stay safe on their adventures

QUALITY: American made, high-end apparel that works as hard as women do, while making them look great, feel great, and perform better

AUTHENTICITY: Loving all body types and women's stories of grace and grit

COMMUNITY: Building a group of awesome, supportive women through our products and programs

As you develop your idea for your new passion project, take the time to identify your ethics. Your list will be different because it is based on your character (a topic we covered in the last chapter), but define your ethics clearly and communicate them to your customers and stakeholders whenever you get the opportunity.

Secrets of Empathy

What does it mean to be empathetic?

- Being curious about other people and imagining what might be going on in their lives.

- Considering what we have in common with someone else and focusing on that instead of what makes us different.

- Asking a lot of questions and listening to the person we are conversing with.

Some of us are more naturally empathetic than others. Your level of empathy depends on all sorts of factors, including how you were raised. If you worry that you might not be as empathetic as you'd like, there is a way to hone your skills: mindfulness training.

Practicing mindfulness is a powerful tool for developing empathy. First and foremost, it is about, getting in touch with yourself. The more in tune you are with yourself, the more in tune you can be with others. Mindfulness training is about building your awareness of the things you might ordinarily take for granted, such as the simple acts of breathing, walking, or sitting. It is also about observing and questioning everything, rather than simply taking something at face value. This includes your emotions and feelings. When we don't take the time to acknowledge and understand our own emotions, we're very unlikely to take the time to do that for others and our ability to empathize is diminished. Mindfulness forces us to exercise that muscle.

Research in neuroscience[12] suggests that there is an area of the brain called the insula that is very important in developing empathy. One study has shown[13] that those practicing meditation and mindfulness have thicker insula. This suggests that mindfulness training significantly changes the brain in ways that improve empathy.

Behavioral science has shown similar findings. A study by researchers at Northeastern University and Gaelle Desbordes of Massachusetts

---

[12] http://www.annualreviews.org/doi/abs/10.1146/annurev-neuro-062111-150536?journalCode=neuro&

[13] https://www.ncbi.nlm.nih.gov/pmc/articles/PMC1361002/

General Hospital, entitled "Meditation Increases Compassionate Responses to Suffering,"[14] describes what happened when a test group was sent on an eight-week mindfulness course, and compared them to a control group who hadn't been trained. In one test, subjects who had been through the meditation training showed more compassion in a waiting room setting to someone on crutches by giving up their seat. Only 16 percent of the control group gave up their seats compared to 50 percent of the test group. The study suggests that only eight weeks of mindfulness training is enough to significantly increase our ability to empathize with another person.

The hardest thing about empathy is that you sometimes must keep your mouth shut and your opinions to yourself. That is sometimes hard for us to do! When you're empathizing with someone, whether they're a friend, family member, colleague, or customer, you can't get into arguments about who is right and who is wrong. Everyone believes they are right (even when the evidence is stacked against them!), and although it's frustrating, try to see it from their point of view. Sometimes, when you ask for feedback from people, you may hear things you don't like.

We want to hear all feedback—good, bad, and in between. Often, a complaint is actually more helpful than a compliment. It helps us to create better products, better experiences, and better processes. However, you also have to become skilled in figuring out who likes to complain for complaining's sake … you almost certainly know someone like this! Not every complaint is justified, but making the complainant feel heard is often all that's needed for them to back off.

In life and in business, you should also be aware of people who like to think they know best. When you begin a project or enterprise, you'll

---

[14] https://pccondon.files.wordpress.com/2013/09/condon-et-al-2013-ps.pdf

hear a lot of, "You know what you should do …" As annoying as this form of input can be, those people are all just trying to help. This should be a good feeling, and you can channel their interest in your business into a more helpful direction, like becoming an investor, which will earn them a seat at the table and the right to bend your ear!

Kimberly can talk about this with authority, because she was once the one saying, "You know what you should do…" when she was a young executive. Her boss at the time, Virgil Gardaya, was a great listener, and when he was done listening to her suggestions for what the company should be doing, he said, "Great. If you can do it better, do it." He gave her control of a very significant portion of the company's revenues. At only twenty-seven years old, Kim was suddenly managing a lot of people, and her boss offered his full mentoring support. Sometimes, empathy is knowing what someone wants or needs before even they know it themselves.

If you think back to your own work experience, you'll probably be able to think of one manager in particular that made a deep impression on you. That boss likely took a deep interest in you and gave you the authority to develop your role. Kate learned a lot from one of her bosses, for whom she worked when she arrived in California. Joe was the head of a nonprofit, and Kate worked for him part-time. When she wanted to work full-time, she proposed the creation of a full-time post. Joe could have just turned her away, but he cared for his staff and their families, so he took the risk and hired her. Together, they made it successful, and Kate built a program that brought in additional revenue. Of course, as the head of a nonprofit, Joe was naturally inclined to be empathetic! He cared a lot for the kids he worked with, and no child was ever turned away.

This level of caring was grace in action.

Enjoyment

Working for an empathetic boss or company makes life a lot more enjoyable. And the people we know who are the most full of grace and grit are those who live life with joy.

Dealing with life with a sense of humor can be incredibly hard, but it's an effective way to get through the gritty moments. In 1927, Freud wrote this in an essay about gallows humor: "The ego refuses to be distressed by the provocations of reality, to let itself be compelled to suffer. It insists that it cannot be affected by the traumas of the external world; it shows, in fact, that such traumas are no more than occasions for it to gain pleasure."

We don't recommend laughing at others' misfortune! But in life, love, and business, the ability to laugh will see you through.

A few years ago, we were attempting to get some legal fundraising documents completed by a deadline. We had to get them in by a certain time, or we would have to pay again the next day to re-submit the paperwork. We were super stressed and focused on completing the task. While we were reviewing the documents, two of our team members (Liz and Sherrie) were stuck in traffic in the midst of a California wildfire. We couldn't hang up on them. They were in a tough situation, and wanted to share the craziness they were living through (as wildfires blazed around their jeep, a man was walking in the middle of the highway offering cupcakes to the stranded cars!). We had less than twenty minutes to complete the documents, and we started laughing at the ridiculousness of their situation. We were anxious to complete our task. To this day, those employees that were helping us don't understand why we were laughing and giggling! Our natural reaction to the crisis was to laugh; it's a lot more fun than crying and a whole lot better for your mental health. However, our timing could have been better.

Appropriate (and, appropriately timed) humor boosts morale. Everyone loves to be around the life and soul of the party.

A lot of businesses recognize the importance of fun, creative environments.—they've worked out that their employees want to spend more time in the workplace! The big technology companies are good at this. Google campuses, for example, are full of artwork and social spaces where employees can play, eat, and meet. It's something that is sniffed at by more traditional companies as being frivolous and pandering to the millennial worker, but staff turnover at these fun-filled companies is much lower.

As a startup, you won't have the resources to spend on a ping-pong table for employees, but you can find small, low- or no-cost ways to have fun with your people. Just be aware that their definition of fun might be a little different than yours! You can even make the everyday tasks of running a business fun. If you check out our **GRACEDBYGRIT** videos and social media, you'll see what we mean: we almost always have a blast!

Of course, your sense of humor is pretty fixed, so it isn't as if you can learn to laugh in the face of adversity if you're not naturally inclined to do so. But there are other ways to show enjoyment and make it through the gritty moments. We're fortunate because we work in a field people tend to enjoy: fitness. Therefore, it's not too hard to add fun to our day and enhance our employees' and customers' lives. The events and programs we have offer fun times. Often, Kate will make everybody fall to the floor for a plank or ab session.

Outside of work, in your daily life, we hope you find enjoyment in the simple things. Your home. Your family. Your dog. Your friends. Practice the mindfulness we talked about earlier in the chapter to recognize and appreciate all the things that give you peace, love, and joy, so that when times get tough, you have all the resources you need to make it through the grit with grace.

To end, we would like to share one final story from a woman we love, Katy Cannata. Her story of grit and grace is about the quest to find joy from the depths of despair. Enjoyment of life can be elusive when we hit hard times, but as Katy shows, just putting one foot in front of the other will pay off. You will find your joy in the end.

A Woman with Joy: Katy Cannata

Hi, I'm Katy. This is my story of why I am **GRACED**BY**GRIT***.*

I was a sensitive child. I have always been deeply impacted by the emotional worlds of those around me. I spent much of my adolescence trying on various roles, but I never had a clear vision of who I was. At twelve, I became the keeper of all things, absorbing my friends' secrets, my mother's sadness, and my father's silent rage. When he floundered, I stepped up as the more reliable, responsible sibling to my older brother, and advised my mother when it was time to leave her failing marriage. Each member of our family was adrift. We waded through the same waters but failed to conjoin. The weight of these emotional worlds anchored me and did little to help me find myself. With no sense of where I belonged but knowing it was never where I was, I left home at eighteen and spent the next eight years wandering through countries, cities, and states looking for home.

By twenty-six, I had landed in a bad marriage. It was the pinnacle of an overdue relationship on which I had pinned the entirety of my self-worth. I could fix this marriage if only I could fix him (that is, make him love me as I loved him, wholeheartedly and without question), and then I would be whole. It would be four more years before I left what would be a decade-long relationship. It was the whole of my twenties, and many more years were spent unpacking why I had stayed as long as I had. At twenty-six though, I was starting to become unhinged. I suffered the physical ramifications of years of untreated anxiety and depression including panic attacks, frequent bouts of hives, excruciating monthly yeast infections, and ulcers in my stomach and mouth. But I wasn't yet ready to quit.

151

I eventually came to realize that leaving the marriage would save my life. I never believed my husband was capable of physically harming me until the night I left. He raged two inches from my face, and something clicked in me. It said, GET OUT NOW. Run for your life, and don't stop. I already had my own apartment, but oh, how I mourned my fairy-tale ending. We are so often conditioned to believe in the shoulds. Our mothers don't have to tell us it's what we want (though mine did) for us to understand where we stand. We should be married by the time we are thirty. We should have kids. We should want all this and fight for it. Any failing of this version of reality is a failing of us—a failing of our worthiness. Oh, we can fight the good feminist fight, but at the end of the day, the prize is still the diamond ring, the coveted proposal. At twenty-six, I believed I had dedicated my best, most attractive years to this man and this relationship. So what if it was no good? Who did I think I was kidding that I could nab another man with so much ambition, with such a good family? So what if he was emotionally and verbally abusive? So what if he made it crystal clear I would never, ever be good enough to be in his inner circle? If I rolled up my sleeves and dug in hard enough, I could make it work.

Maybe it was the dawning of a new decade, but at thirty years old I glimpsed a different life. It wasn't glamorous; I had no money and was in debt. I wasn't even sure it was a happier life than the one I was leaving. I was desperate not to be alone, and had no idea how to be on my own. But something deep inside my soul told me that there was another way. My gritty moment was putting one foot in front of the other. A new city wasn't far enough—I needed a new coast. I fled west for the second time in my life, making half-hearted promises to the perfectly-good-enough job and a perfectly-nice-enough new boyfriend that I would be back in a year, promises I would break before my feet settled into the cold and cleansing water of the San Diego shoreline.

The shoulds still haunted me. It was unrealistic in this economy to leave behind a good paying job. I was chasing the sun. I had no plan. I was in debt. All of this was true, of course. For the first year, I worked in a coffee shop where I learned to make lattes. Then I worked as a hostess in a kitschy hotel bar, flirting with salty guests who sank into bar stools and drank cucumber-garnished libations.I tried to ignore the fact that I couldn't work weddings without developing debilitating anxiety; my own special concoction of self-hatred and tears. I tried on various versions of myself once more. I drank too much and passed out in precarious situations more often than I care to remember. I made more mistakes. But I took my time. I started going to therapy (free sessions given by graduate students who left at the end of each semester). I wrote, page after page of nonsense and poetry. I read books on happiness and dutifully did the enclosed workbook pages. I did yoga. I started to run. I watched the sun set over the ocean with hundreds of strangers who lined the shore night after night without fail. I tried to move more slowly. I tried to unlearn all the damage he and I had done. I tried to forget the patterns of pain and self-destruction that had taken years to master.

Two years later I met Paul. I had landed a teaching job in San Diego, a huge accomplishment in a city full of transplants. Jobs were scarce, and I was feeling confident and coming into my own. Paul was everything my husband had not been. He was older, accomplished, and artistic, but deeply selfish. I was completely taken with him. With his help, I came to believe that I didn't really want a marriage or kids (those old-fashioned ideals) because he didn't want those things. Paul would suddenly become deeply interested in people or ideas but discarded these passing fads just as quickly. I desperately wanted to be interesting enough for him, but I was barely holding on. When he ended things two days before the new school year began, I was newly in pieces. The old familiar feelings came creeping back. I would never be enough for love. And just like that, I sunk to my knees.

A few months later, I found out I was losing my job. The breakup had devastated me, so much so that I had lost my sense of joy and purpose. It had taken a toll on my job performance. Coupled with a new, no-nonsense boss who needed to prove her own worth, my contract was rescinded for the following year. Everything I had worked for was crashing down. Worse, I might have to leave San Diego, a place that had become my refuge and my home.

When my mettle was tested, I did the one thing I knew I could do. I put one foot in front of the other. At times of great difficulty, I tend to become introspective. I knew I had lost my way. I knew I had to throw myself into something wholeheartedly, with singular devotion, in which I could depend on no one but myself. I needed to develop some self-discipline. Marathon training seemed like just the thing. Once, long ago, I had told my husband I wanted to someday run a marathon. Not even a casual runner at the time, he had laughed in my face. But the idea stuck with me. The thing about running is there's no equipment, no team. It's just you, the road, and whatever grit you brought with you. Training provided me with some of the consistency I had lacked in my upbringing. It tested me. I had recently met someone new, someone who showed promise, but this journey was about me. No one else was going to do the work. Every day I logged my miles. Through heat waves and fighting back tears, through anxiety so crippling at times I could barely breathe, I put one foot in front of the other. I followed my training as if my life depended on it, and I was pretty sure it did. During the day I taught, I made connections, I set up interviews, and I loved my students the best I could to make up for the disservice I felt I had done them. But at night, I ran. It was all I could do to stay standing.

In April, I landed a job at another area school. I had been interviewing far up the California coast, in the mountains of Idyllwild, and even in Hawaii, and once again I received what felt like a windfall. I got to stay in San Diego. And amazingly, somewhere along the way I had built the healthiest relationship of my life. Aaron, a lifetime runner, had casually started doing miles with me. It soon became clear that he too was training for his first marathon. Running was a powerful force in our relationship. As we logged our miles, each week increasing in difficulty, our sights set on the long haul, we worked at something bigger than ourselves. This became a metaphor for our relationship. After months of training, we crossed the finish line together, but we each had found our own way there. And although he made it clear he was committed to going wherever I landed in my new job, we were both thrilled it was San Diego. Finally, I felt I could put down roots. Two years later, Aaron and I were married. A year after that we had our daughter, Juniper Winter.

Now, three months into her life, Juniper is the light of my life, but I still struggle with my demons. In the past year, my husband and I married, started a business, bought a home, and brought a child into the world. The latest marathon has ended, and I find myself asking, what's next? Will I learn to live in the small moments of my life? Can I learn to just be rather than longing to be someone and somewhere I am not, as I have my whole life? Can I be fully present in these glorious, fleeting moments with my child? Can I finally find the courage to love what I do professionally, or do something else? Can I be the mom I want to be? Can I break the old, destructive patterns that still haunt me? Can I learn to love myself the way Aaron loves me, or the way I love Juniper? This is the work I must do now. I have thrived in the gritty moments that life has to offer. Now, I am learning to live in the happy ones.

GRITBOOK **Reflections on Empathy & Enjoyment**

Here we are! Our last opportunity for reflection.

The final exercise is in mindfulness. Simply set aside five minutes for quiet meditation during which you think of all the things that brought you joy today (if you're meditating in the evening) or the previous day (if you're meditating in the morning). Note down below (or in your journal) the joyful things you thought of, and anything you found challenging about the meditation. Over time, this practice will get easier. You may eventually find you're more relaxed as you begin or end your day.

Go Forth with **GRACE & GRIT!**

We are so thankful that you have read our book and shared our story: many of you are part of it. We hope that each of you will learn from what we've learned and go out and be your best self, confront your fears, and build that business. Get out there and do it! The world needs more women running businesses, as does our economy.

We would love to be part of your story. Join our **GRACEDBYGRIT** community—be part of a powerful team that inspires women. Our customers would love to learn about your graceful and gritty stories, so please share them on our blog!

Also, the first twenty people who post inspirational quotes on our Facebook page will receive a surprise item from us.

It has been a fantastic five years. Our children are teenagers now. We are a bit older and we still train together. We see so many women with dreams. We want to help them start their business, take the next step in their career, build a non-profit, run an event or just be an incredible parent or partner. We hope this book will inspire you to take the leap. Don't wait three years like we did: start something now and start it with passion, purpose, and grit.

As we complete this book, we are in the midst of a pivot ourselves. We have struggled to raise enough money to take this company to the level to compete with the biggest players in the market. We believe in this business. We believe in the power of women. We are tough, adaptable, and ready to continue to activate the power within every woman by creating the athletic apparel she needs to feel confident and get things done. It is scary, but we are resilient.

> **"I am not lucky. You know what I am? I am smart,**
> **I am talented, I take advantage of the opportunities**
> **that come my way and I work really, really hard.**
> **Don't call me lucky. Call me a badass."**

Shonda Rhimes

In Honor of the King Family

When the King family had the shattering revelation in late February of 2010 that their little girl Chelsea would never come home, they found the strength to draft and enact laws that now provide protection for more than 17 million kids. They created the sunflower scholarship program which has awarded over $650,000 to amazing students heading off to college, as their daughter dreamt of. Now, they have formed an organization meant to be the voice for our nation's children. In every State Capital building, in Congress, in the Senate, and in the White House, they will be legislating laws to protect our children. They call it "Protect the Joy." Both a rally cry and a mission statement in one, but most importantly it's a reminder of childhood's essence: joy. Finally, there will be a voice to protect it.

If you'd like to learn more or register your support, please visit
www.protectthejoy.org

Afterword & Acknowledgments

The GRACEDBYGRIT Story Continues

By Kimberly Caccavo

On June 1, 2018, we sold the assets of **GRACEDBYGRIT** to HYLETE. While I remain an investor in the new company, I am no longer working on the day-to-day business. This has given me time to reflect on the company that Kate and I built and the team of young women we helped to shape.

What an incredible experience it has been for each of us. Eight years ago, Kate and I were on a run talking about the benefits of wearing great-fitting women's athletic apparel. We wanted safety, fit, and performance. We wanted to look good while exercising. I had business experience; Kate was a trainer and an athlete. We had each been through that gritty moment that could make or break us, and those moments defined each of us. I saw something in Kate; she had so much to offer, yet was using only a small fraction of her potential. She had experience starting athletic and organizational businesses and had always been a leader, but she hadn't had the opportunity to push herself to be all that she could be. We waited too long after that first run to start **GRACEDBYGRIT,** but I am glad we did. I was so lucky to watch Kate mature and develop into an excellent leader.

Kate got experience the hard (and FUN) way. In the course of running our company, we accomplished so many great things together. We started a business based on a loyal and active community. We built and rebuilt a website. We designed over 90 products. We found fabrics, manufacturers, labels, and packaging. We held almost 500 trunk shows/ Fit Shops, and trained teens at our **GRITTY**GIRLS sessions. We opened a retail store and had five retail pop-ups. We had over $3.5 million in lifetime revenue, 40,000 customers, over 400 influencers, and over 100 partnerships. Our business was featured in *Shape, Women's Wear Daily, Forbes, Health, InStyle, Self, Huffington Post* and so many other publications. But, more than all that, we giggled, we laughed, we yelled, we stressed, we sweated … we had the most wonderful experience of our lives. Together.

I am so excited to see what the next step is for Kate. She is an excellent executive, a hard worker and incredibly smart. Her speaking abilities are phenomenal. One of my favorite things is how great she became videotaping and creating content for our website. She is a natural. She might even have a future in television.

The most amazing accomplishment was the team of women we assembled. Our team was talented, passionate, determined, and committed to making **GRACED**BY**GRIT** the premier athletic apparel company for women. We hired women from every walk of life at different stages in their development. We worked so hard together: laughing, crying, traveling, and creating. It was so gratifying to see each of them grow and develop their skills and confidence. We watched proudly as they moved to the next phase of their lives.

Kayli Fraser was our first employee. Smart, organized, and determined, she went from intern to leader quickly. On her way there, she tested clothing, moved boxes, catalogued photos, kept up on social media, and became our store manager. When we wanted to test our fabric in the ocean, we sent Kayli out on a stand-up paddle board. She never complained. She did what was asked and did it well. She even held herself back from rolling her eyes when Kate and I dissolved into fits of giggles as we filled out our incorporation documents. Early on, when we had issues with another company, Kayli did research and found out that they were incorrect. She worked tirelessly with us for four years.

Ralene Cavataio was the mom of one of my son's grade school friends. She had been the CFO at Sally Ride Science. When we told her we were starting an athletic apparel company, she offered her help. She helped us create our first documents and incorporate the company. She was with us from the beginning and stayed until the very end. Ralene was our go to person for all things financial and HR.

Liz Lawson was the employee that didn't want to be an employee. She did not want a job. She was retired. Or so she thought. She can't help herself—when Liz sees a problem, she wants to fix it. She organized us, packed for Fit Shops, organized the office, and kept us running smoothly. She organized zippers, trim, and all of our production. It wasn't enough to just organize us; she went to our manufacturers and took sleepy, family-run businesses and helped transform them to make them more efficient to compete with China for production. She worked hard. She worked weekends. She worked nights. Liz's daughter ran for a local high school. We had her test our shorts, and when she went to University of Washington, she helped us with Fit Shops in the Seattle area. She would assist her mom when needed. If that wasn't enough, Liz got her husband Bill involved. Together, they packed and moved inventory from our manufacturers to third-party logistics to our pop-up shops back to our main store. She had Bill repair the company Jeep, fix broken tents, and patch walls in the store. She worked hard and loved it.

Sherrie Bainer was our first model, first online customer, and biggest fan. She wore our outfits and assumed the gritty attitude of our clothes. But it wasn't a big stretch. Sherrie is made of grit. She worked at Qualcomm, a local company. She would come over after work or on her lunch break to help the team out. She purchased clothes for birthdays, graduations, anniversaries...you name it. When we decided to shift our effort and try to go into retail establishments, we hired Sherrie to help lead the charge. She went one step further and ran our sales for two years. The stores, customers and our team loved her. So do we. She was a passionate and enthusiastic employee, friend and customer.

Chevigny Brady moved to San Diego to find out if a relationship would work. She was ambitious and was learning new things as fast as we could train her. She worked in our shipping department and helped send out our product with loving care to our customers. She was also on the phone with customers, helping them with their problems. She became our fit model and contributed to the styles we created. She worked with our third-party logistics company and managed inventory. When we decided to re-launch our website, she worked with the developers and learned how to run it on Magento. When we shifted the website to Shopify, Chev was right there, ready and willing to help. She managed the build out, learned to code, and speak the language of our developers. She is smart, talented, and on the up and up.

Jessica Brown started working in customer service and as our office manager. She filed papers, kept passwords, helped with accounts receivable, and kept the office running smoothly. But, Jessica Brown is an artist. When we needed a new pattern for a pair of leggings, we asked Jessica to design something that resembled something amphibious. She came up with our iconic mermaid leggings. We had to reprint them about twenty times. People love them. Jessica decided to apply her artistry to photography. She started with small in-office shoots and graduated to producing and creatively managing full-blown sessions. When she left us, she was hired by a sock company to shoot photos for their marketing campaigns.

We had a group of local moms that loved our product. They hosted Fit Shops in their homes, but wanted to get more involved. **Kelly Miller**, **Cielo Porreco**, **Jen Baumgartner**, and **Danielle Egan** gave up time in their days to work our store and share our message with our local San Diego customers. We called them the **Cardiff Moms** because they all lived in a town called Cardiff. They were essential in building a strong community of women who supported each other no matter if they were working or stay-at-home moms. Their humor and helpfulness made the store an incredibly happy place to visit.

A few of our interns loved the company so much they later became full-time employees:

Sarah Andersen offered to work for free, so she could build community and learn about an athletic apparel company. She was a Yogi and a life coach. She worked so hard on each of her projects that we realized we needed her on our team. Sarah joined us and went from trunk show/ Fit Shop salesperson to developing and running our GRITTYGIRLS program. Her gift is working with teenage girls and teaching them about grit. She also shows them that their imperfections are often their biggest strengths.

Alex Vidaeff was enthusiastic and willing to try anything. She flew out from Michigan on her own, set up an apartment and worked diligently over the summer. During her senior year of college, she continued to work for us from the University of Michigan. We felt so blessed and lucky to have her on our team that we offered her a full-time job. She jumped in and proved to be incredible. We used her when we created the application for our StartEngine fundraising campaign, Shark Tank, and a lot of the marketing assets that we used from day to day. We were so proud of her when she landed a job in Los Angeles doing a little bit of everything she learned at **GRACED**BY**GRIT**.

Mariah Fuller joined us from a local university. When she graduated, she came to work in the store where she became a point person for marketing information. Mariah's constant smile and dedication to the work we were doing was so fabulous. She worked in the store and the office; email campaigns became her specialty, and she figured out how to run them all on her own. We were so blessed to have her.

Alessa Blackwell is blessed with features that make her look 16. A group of us were having cocktails one day, and I wasn't going to serve her. She then informed me that she was 30 years old! She brought calm and order to our team during a critical pop-up store in Carlsbad. That same calm and order translated to running customer service. Every call and email was met with her ability to figure anything out and turn a customer's frustration into a smile.

Abigail Blackert interned for us during her last term at the Fashion Institute in Chicago. We were so impressed with her attention to detail and desire to work hard. Communicating with factories and vendors became her strength, and contractors loved her as much as we do. She surprised us all with how easily she became a two-stepping San Diego woman.

There were so many other employees and people that helped us along the way. **Lucy Delagarza** was preparing to have her second child when she helped us through our first prototypes and our first run of production. **Kay Sickafoose** jumped in and helped set up our website in the beginning. **Aaron Nowlan**, Kate's ex-husband, also helped with the website and even helped put our store together late into the night before opening. **Annie Adams** joined us from ASICS to help with sales. **Vivian Havenner** joined us with a baby on her hip—we all got to watch that baby, and her second, learn to crawl, talk, and walk. **Mindy Service** will be forever in our hearts; as we eat a slice of bread, we will think of her incredible work ethic. **Emma Beckstrom** joined us as an intern, helped us with our first crowdfunding campaign and returned to help Chevigny change our web platform. **Cheyne McQuisten** also helped through many stages of our journey; he carried countless boxes, learned to replace car batteries and became an expert in heat transfer applications. We giggle when we remember this incredible surf instructor and property manager removing and replacing pads in our sports bras so he could apply the logos with our heat transfer machine. He was a trooper!

Our incredible and hard-working vendors quickly became a part of the **GRACEDBYGRIT** family. **Luca Ferrari** provided the most luxurious fabrics and visited our office and welcomed the chaos and humor. **Kathleen Goertzen** created markers and patterns. She added her vast experience and expertise in fittings and with the storytelling that always took place. **Jesus** at Smart Cutting was a man of his word— he reminded us that lunch hour is a time to enjoy food, the people around us and to take a pause at work. He also proved that a handshake deal still exists. **Shashi and Shay Pal** of Indu Fashions welcomed us to their factory where they sewed our products with grace and beauty. They have proven that American manufacturing is still alive, and all the women that wear the product appreciate the quality and precision that goes into their work.

Our children were also involved from the very beginning, living the day to day with moms that were busy working away and often very tired. Kate's two gorgeous and smart daughters **Maggi Nowlan** and

Gwen Nowlan have modeled for us and worked events, the store, and set up pop up shops. My son, **Christopher Caccavo**, is an excellent water photographer who took shots of our models stand-up paddling, surfing, and hanging out on the beach. We used so many of his photos for marketing and advertising. My daughter, **Grace Caccavo**, modeled for us, sorted zippers, clothes, and tagged the items. She helped whenever she could. So did **Haley Bainer, Kate Miller, Riley Baumgartner, Iliana Porreco, Cece,** and **Josie Egan.**

The numerous members of our families, extended families, and dear friends near and far that hosted events, attended events, and sacrificed their time to help is incredible. Their support and generosity in providing meals, beds to sleep in, and the faith in our vision and brand simply because they believed in us has made us forever grateful.

There is one person whose help was invaluable: my generous, gracious, and super-intelligent husband **Jim Caccavo**. He helped us with the business plan, financials, relationships in the apparel business and served on our board. He also funded the company. He gave of his money, his time, and, most importantly, of his heart. I am forever grateful.

Each person we worked with helped shape our company. We are so thankful for what each of them brought to our team. We leave a legacy of inclusivity among women. It creates power, strength, and support that we hope inspires future generations to make it happen. We have proven that a team of women can make a huge difference in the lives of others and can build a GREAT company.

Kimberly Caccavo

Co-Founder and CEO, **GRACEDBYGRIT**

Kimberly brought technology and business experience to **GRACEDBYGRIT**. She received her BS in Chemical Engineering from UC Berkeley and an MBA from UCLA. She has had a rich and varied career during which she designed metals used in the space shuttle; did research on ceramic heat engines; ran a telephone directory business; helped privatize a Latin American phone company; started a cable company; worked in Hollywood; and had her own consultancy helping launch businesses.

Kimberly has been **GRACEDBYGRIT** many times. As a kid, she helped her single mom balance a checkbook; she married young and was widowed; she survived a kidnapping attempt; and now she is graced with a great business background and an entertaining family that keeps her on her toes. Kimberly is married to Jim Caccavo and has two teenage children.

Kate Nowlan

Former Co-Founder and COO, **GRACED**BY**GRIT** and Current VP of Brand Experience, HYLETE

Kate brought coaching experience and product knowledge specific to female athletes to **GRACED**BY**GRIT**. Kate is now the VP of Brand Experience for HYLETE. She is a natural people-person and loves working with a team to make it happen.

Kate received her BA in Sociology and Psychology from UMass Amherst. As an entrepreneur, she owned her own company organizing small businesses and homes. She launched, coached, and grew a youth and masters swim program, was an executive for a nonprofit in which she planned and ran events, coordinated fundraisers, ran the day-to-day office operations, and launched new revenue-driving community programs. Her experience as an athlete and a running and swim coach, fundraising executive, and entrepreneur have taught her to constantly think of ways to improve efficiency and results.

Kate has also been **GRACED**BY**GRIT**. She became a mom at 21 while still in college; she was divorced at 30 and became a single mom. She is now graced by an incredible family, boyfriend and career. Kate is raising two teenage daughters in Encinitas, CA, and enjoys spending quality time with those she loves, usually outside enjoying the Southern California sunshine and breathing the ocean air.

40615817R00100

Made in the USA
San Bernardino, CA
27 June 2019